They spring at you from the television.

They are born from bar bets.

They come to you in dreams and gnaw at your brain into the wee hours of the morning.

They are the sometimes absurd, often obsessive questions that have plagued humanity since the beginning of history.

They are the questions of the curious.

JUST CURIOUS ABOUT HISTORY, Jeeves®

Jack Mingo & Erin Barrett

With Illustrations by Marcos Sorensen and Spence Snyder

POCKET BOOKS

New York   London   Toronto   Sydney   Singapore

An *Original* Publication of POCKET BOOKS

POCKET BOOKS, a division of Simon & Schuster, Inc.
1230 Avenue of the Americas, New York, NY 10020

ISBN: 0-7434-2709-2

First Pocket Books trade paperback printing January 2002

10   9   8   7   6   5   4   3   2   1

POCKET and colophon are registered trademarks of
Simon & Schuster, Inc.

For information regarding special discounts for bulk purchases,
please contact Simon & Schuster Special Sales at 1-800-456-6798
or business@simonandschuster.com

Cover design by Gregg Loew; front cover illustration by Marcos
Sorensen and Spence Snyder

Printed in the U.S.A.

ACKNOWLEDGMENTS

Special thanks to:

Amanda Ayers
Paolo Pepe
Donna O'Neill
Kathlyn McGreevy
Marcos Sorensen
Spencer Snyder
Penny Finnie
Kathy Lowenstern
Steve Berkowitz
John Dollison
Anne Kinney
Jerry & Lynn Barrett
Elana Mingo
Eric Childs
Georgia Hamner
Jackson Hamner

CONTENTS

FROM THE AUTHORS

In a way, it's a shame they teach history in school because they ruin it. How much do you remember from lectures, the timelines of history, and the overstuffed textbooks? Yeah, that's about how much we remember, too.

The problem is that the history books leave out the good stuff. It doesn't have to be that way, of course. History unvarnished is as fascinating as any bestseller, since it's full of the same stuff that makes a good read: conflict, blood, jealousy, rivalries, tenderness, heroes and dupes, villains and scoundrels, tragedy, and a whole lot of unintentional comedy.

Did you know that Egyptian doctors used wooden mallets to render patients unconscious for surgery? That some of the worst plagues in history came after superstitious Europeans killed cats as witches, allowing the rats to run free? Or that Attila the Hun died making love, not war?

Okay, so maybe some of these things weren't exactly knee-slappers at the time, but at least they're good for a chuckle or a knowing smirk now. And really, what else could anybody ask for?

We were thrilled when we were asked to write more books after the first volume of Just Curious, Jeeves. We love the process of finding out what people want to know, the questions that people ask for no reason other than that they are "just curious." As we began thinking about writing this book, we went to our special source of inspiration: the secret backstage "peek box" at "Ask Jeeves." It's the place where we can watch the incoming questions as they whiz by at a dizzying rate.

Ask!

How does the "Ask Jeeves" search engine work?

As you may know, "Ask Jeeves" is one of the most popular websites on the Internet. An average of 2.7 gazillion questions roll in every single day of the year. True, many of them are fairly basic questions ("How do I bake a ham?"; "Where can I buy cheap plane tickets?"; "How can I find nude pictures of that sexy movie star Don Knotts?"). For those, we just stay out of the way and watch the computerized butler handle them with his customary deftness, combining the labors of flesh-and-blood helpers with the magic of high-speed computers.

When we were at the peek box, we looked for the unexpected questions, the ones that got us wondering, too. We especially liked the ones that asked for quirky historical details like, "What's the oldest restaurant in the world?"; "Was Doc Holliday really a doctor?", and so on. Whether the questions came from somebody just thinking about stuff in the middle of the night, wagering on a bar bet, or trying to show up a know-it-all big brother, these are the questions that piqued our interest and inspired us to go out and find answers.

And so over several months we did exactly that. Now we're eager to share with you what we've learned. Stuff like how long a head stays conscious after being removed by a guillotine (about 15 seconds) and the return address Jack the Ripper wrote on his letters to the police ("From Hell"). We now know which founding father was eaten by an apple tree (Roger Williams) and what Walt Whitman's day job was (clerk in Lincoln's Indian Department). We've learned how many wars and near-wars were started by pigs (at least four, including the Hatfield–McCoy feud); why the Chihuahua was bred (warmth and food); and what to never, never bring up in conversation with the eunuchs from the Chinese Royal Court (dogs without tails, for one).

If you were sleeping or passing notes in history class, here's a chance to catch up on some of what you missed. Even if you were paying attention, here's a bunch of history they probably never told you. Enjoy, and keep asking those questions!

Just Curious About History,

THE WILD, WILD WEST

The Old West was a legendary period in American history—in fact, so legendary that some of it has become more legend than truth. But grab your spurs and saddle up Ol' Paint, pardner, and let's try to set the record straight.

A COWBOY NEEDS A HORSE

What are jinglebobs, heel chains, and rowels?

They're parts of a cowboy's spurs.

Did cowboys wear high heels to make them look taller?

Well, maybe in some of the movie cowboys. The real-life kind, however, wore them for two reasons: to keep their feet from slipping out of the stirrups and to put some extra distance between their feet and the muck when walking through fields full of cattle excrement.

How much water can a ten-gallon hat hold?

About three quarts. So, how did it get its name, you may well ask? Some say it was just a cowboy exaggeration about the size of the hat, but those who claim to know say that it's because the hat was advertised as being big enough for 10 *galions*. (Galions are those braids that decorated the crown.) Regardless, what most people don't know is that this classic cowboy hat style was first manufactured by John B. Stetson in that Wild West town of Philadelphia, Pennsylvania.

Why were cowboys called cowpokes or cowpunchers?

Because poke and punch is what they literally did to cattle that balked at going up the ramps leading to railcars and packing plants.

> **How many cowboys were African American?**
> About ¼. Another ¼ were Mexican.

Where did the Old West ranchers get their horses and cattle if they didn't transport them from back East?

Both mustangs and Texas longhorns ran wild through the plains when the first settlers moved west. It was just a matter of catching and domesticating them. Neither animal, though, was indigenous to the Americas—they were descended from animals that had been brought over to Mexico by Spaniards in the 1500s. Over the intervening three centuries, feral herds of horses and longhorns had grazed their way up and across the continent.

WHEN IT ABSOLUTELY NEEDS TO GET THERE IN A FORTNIGHT

How long did it take to get a letter from coast to coast by Pony Express?

In the middle of the 1800s, before the U.S. got wired with telegraph, you'd send a piece of mail from the East Coast to the West and not expect it to get there for months. A simple mail exchange of "Here's the contract; do we have a deal?" could require a half year or more before you got a response. In the frontier beyond the Mississippi River, there were no trains, not even roads to speak of, and most mail either went over land on a creeping stagecoach or by ship around South America.

People in business, government, and journalism hated waiting that long. So you could see how the Pony Express really seemed like a brilliant idea at the time. Your package was absolutely, positively guaranteed to get the nearly 2,000 miles from Sacramento to St. Louis in 10 days (15 in winter). Even adding a few more days for the trains to take your message the rest of the way to business centers in New York or Chicago, you can still see how a one-month turnaround time could be an exciting prospect.

That's how William Russell saw it anyway when the idea of the Central Overland Pony Express Company came to him. In order to have mail traveling at the fastest possible speed—of horses galloping in a relay race against time—he realized that was going to take hundreds of horses, scores of riders, and stations at reasonable intervals to trade horses and riders (horses every 10–15 miles, riders every 75). He also knew that traveling through Indian territory would be dangerous. He figured that he'd have to charge a bundle per letter to make it worth his while, but he hoped that would come down once he got the government contracts.

It cost $5 per half-ounce to send a package by Pony Express in 1860, which is the equivalent of about $95 in today's dollars. Despite the outrageous cost, the Pony Express still lost money on every letter it carried. Worst of all, the government contracts founder William Russell expected never materialized. With some relief, Russell closed the whole thing down two days after the first coast-to-coast telegraph line went online. In its 19 months of existence, the Pony Express delivered 34,753 pieces of mail and ended up nearly $200,000 in debt.

How many Pony Express riders were killed by Indians, outlaws, etc.?

It was a dangerous job, as indicated by the newspaper ads that recruited riders: "Wanted: Young, skinny, wiry fellows. Not over 18. Must be expert riders. Willing to risk death daily. Orphans preferred." Surprisingly, though, the 183 riders (aged 11 through the mid-40s, despite the ad) survived pretty well. Only one was killed by Indians, although his pony knew the way and continued with the mail to the next station. For the danger, the riders were paid $100–150 a month (equivalent to about $1,900–2,750 in today's money).

Ask! Where can I read about the history of the Pony Express?

EAST IS WEST & EVER THE TRAIN SHALL MEET

Before the transcontinental railroad was completed, how were goods shipped to the western territories?

Some were carried across country, but it was an expensive and overly difficult task, coming across mountainous regions and prairie terrain. The easier, although far more distant, route west was by sea. Almost all goods, including those used to start work on the transcontinental railroad, were shipped around Cape Horn and across thousands of statute miles to reach western American destinations. The only transcontinental railroad building materials naturally found on the West Coast were timber (for various structures and cross ties), stone, and brick. Tools, rail, appliances, machines, and many of the laborers had to be shipped in from other locations.

Did slaves work on the transcontinental railroad?

No. By the time work began in the 1860s, the Civil War was already raging and slavery was on its way out. Instead, two work crews began laying track from the two ends of the railroad line, and they met in Utah. The laborers from the east were mostly Irish and the ones from the west, mostly Chinese.

When was the last rail laid on the transcontinental railroad?
May 10, 1869.

HOW'S TRICKS?

What did the Native American word "how" mean, "How are ya?"

No, but good guess. You're not far off from what it's come to mean for most American movie watchers. "How," or something sounding similar, came from the language of the Sioux tribe. The word was used at the beginning of their sentences in the same way we would say, "Well," and then trounce off into a thought. Settlers may have misinterpreted and thought they were saying "hello." Or even, "How are ya?"

DO NOT FORSAKE ME, OH MY DARLIN'

How often did gunmen do the Main Street quick-draw shoot-out duel like you see in the movies?

Not nearly as often as in the movies. In fact, there isn't a single documented case of it ever happening like the movies portray it. The whole quick-draw myth came from early dime novels. When Wyatt Earp was asked about quick-draw shoot-outs in the 1920s, he told an interviewer that the guy who drew his gun and shot quickly invariably missed. The way to survive a gunfight, Earp said, was to take a second before shooting to steady your hand and aim.

How dangerous was it to live in a Wild West town?

Not as dangerous as you'd think. As a matter of fact, the modern-day cliché of using the Wild West as a metaphor for the dangers of big cities does a grave disservice to the olden days. Take wild, wild Dodge City. Its absolutely worst year for violence was 1878; the total number of shooting deaths that year was five. Combine the shooting deaths for *all* of the cattle towns from 1870 to 1885, and you'll get a total of 45.

My great-grandmother told me she saw a bloody shoot-out in Nevada in the late 1800s. How come I can't find any record of it?

It could be that she fell for a small-town hoax. During the 1870s, Palisades, Nevada, got a reputation as one tough little town because train passengers on rest stops there often witnessed stagecoach robberies, shoot-outs, and even Indian attacks. In reality, though, it was all a big joke. A conductor had once mentioned to a Palisades resident that his passengers were disappointed that the Wild West wasn't like they'd read about in dime novels. The townspeople decided to give the greenhorns what they wanted. They recruited members of the community, the railroad workers, and even a local Indian tribe to join in. Over the next three years, the locals thrilled travelers with a thousand fake gunfights, using blanks and gallons of beef blood from a local slaughterhouse. Palisades got the reputation for being a dangerous town, and sometimes even got written up in newspapers by journalists who weren't in on the joke. Behind the façade, though, Palisades was so peaceful that it didn't even have a sheriff.

WESTWARD SLOW

How fast could covered wagon trains travel?

One to two miles per hour, or the equivalent of a toddler's walking speed. They could go about a hundred miles in a seven-day week of travel, but many devout people refused to travel on Sunday, slowing them down even further.

What's a "dogie"?

It's what they used to call a motherless calf. Stray calves or those that have lost their mothers at too young an age are still called dogies, actually. Often the term is colloquially used to refer to all bovine in a herd. The origin of the word "dogie" is unknown, but may stem from an earlier descriptive term of a motherless calf with an extended belly from malnutrition, says the *American Heritage Dictionary of the English Language* (Fourth Edition, 2000). These hungry calves were once referred to as "dough-guts" because their bellies resembled bulging sacks of sour dough.

What was the average speed of a cattle drive?

Not that much faster than a wagon train. Fifteen miles in a day was pretty typical as the cowboys moved the dogies toward a railroad stop where the cattle could be shipped for slaughter in eastern slaughterhouses. Until the railroad lines reached the western frontier, cattle drives could travel as far as a thousand miles and last up to three months.

What was the speed of a stagecoach?

The fastest way to get across the plains was by stagecoach. Traveling day and night, you could rip through about 100 miles per day—an average of a little more than four miles an hour.

FRONTIER JUSTICE

Who was the judge who fined a corpse $40 for carrying a concealed weapon?

That would be Judge Roy Bean, who liked to call himself "the law west of the Pecos." He presided over his jurisdiction from his combination court and barroom in Langtry, Texas. An article in *Smithsonian Magazine* characterized his unschooled judging as "unfettered by legalities and governed by simple greed, prejudice, and rough-handed common sense." When he discovered that a corpse was carrying both a gun and $40, Bean confiscated the money, explaining that he could use it better than the corpse could. He often interrupted trials to ask if anybody in the courthouse wanted to buy a drink.

ROOTIN' TOOTIN' COWGAL

Who was Calamity Jane?

She was a woman who lived on the Western Frontier in the late 1800s. She was a controversial character for a number of reasons, including the fact that she dressed in men's clothes. She was known to loudly boast of her stint as a Pony Express rider and about serving under General Custer. Some of her life stories have been verified by others or by public record, but because she was known for exaggerating, it can safely be said that many stories about Calamity Jane aren't true. She was often forgiven her white lies because of her big heart. Besides being an ever loyal and faithful friend to many, including Wild Bill Hickock, she also selflessly stayed in Deadwood, South Dakota, during a particularly vicious wave of smallpox and almost single-handedly nursed the community back to health, risking her own health in the process. She joined Buffalo Bill's traveling show for a time, but alcoholism made her an unreliable act, and she was eventually fired. She died near Deadwood in poverty and was buried next to Wild Bill Hickock.

What was Calamity Jane's real name?

She was born Martha Jane Canary. She added "Burke" to that and went by "Martha" or "M. Burke" during her marriage to a man named Clinton Burke, but she dropped it after abandoning him. Her nickname, "Calamity Jane," before and after her marriage was her name of choice. By 1902 she lived down to her name and died after years of alcoholism.

Did Calamity Jane have kids?

Her autobiography says she had a daughter with her husband Clinton Burke. However, her daughter's name is unknown, as is her eventual fate.

Was "Oakley" Annie's real last name or a stage name?

It was a stage name, as was the "Annie," too. Her real name was Phoebe Moses, and she was born in Darke County, Ohio. Another stage name she used in advertisements was "Little Sure Shot." The famous Native American chief Sitting Bull gave the name to her, after being wowed at her marksmanship. As was common for the day, she privately went by her husband's name, Mrs. Frank Butler.

Ask! What did Annie Oakley look like?

I SHALL FEAR NO EVIL

Who named Death Valley and why?

A group of pioneers dubbed it Death Valley in 1849 after they were seriously misrouted there on their way to California's Gold Country. As they finally escaped the valley, one of the women turned around and shouted, "Goodbye, Death Valley!" The name stuck. Despite the name, though, only one of their members actually died in Death Valley—an ailing old man who probably would've died no matter where they'd been. An irony is that the group that named it wasn't afraid of dying from the heat. Although summer temperatures in Death Valley can be deadly, this group arrived in the valley on Christmas Day and it was freezing. They were mostly afraid that they'd be stranded like the Donner Party had been three years earlier.

MMM, TASTES LIKE MR. WOLFINGER

How many people were eaten in the Donner Party?

It was a desperate situation. Trying to get to California, 90 people left too late, gambled on the weather holding, and lost. They were trapped in the Sierra Nevada by winter snows. Separated into several groups, stuck from November until April, they began eating their dead when the food ran out. Forty-eight people survived; of that number, at least half had engaged in cannibalism. Of those who died, nearly all were at least partially eaten. Yum.

Lewis Keseberg was unlucky enough to be the sole survivor of one group. His wife and child had gone with an earlier rescue expedition, and after he had eaten twigs and everything he could find from the provisions, he waited four days before he decided, for his family's sake, that he'd better try eating the bodies of his fellow travelers. "The necessary mutilation of the bodies of those who had been my friends, rendered the ghastliness of my situation more frightful," he recounted to an author in 1880 after 36 years of pained silence. "The flesh of starved beings contains little nutriment. It is like feeding straw to horses. I cannot describe the unutterable repugnance with which I tasted the first mouthful of flesh." For two months he was the only living being in the snowed-in cabin. "Five of my companions had died . . . and their stark and ghastly bodies lay there day and night, seemingly gazing at me with their glazed and staring eyes. I was too weak to remove them. . . . To have one's suffering prolonged inch by inch, to be deserted, forsaken, hopeless; to see that loathsome food ever before my eyes was almost too much for human endurance. . . . Many a time I had the muzzle of my pistol in my mouth and my finger on the trigger, but the faces of my helpless, dependent wife and child would rise up before me, and my hand would fall powerless. . . . I am conversant with four different languages, yet in all four I do not find words enough to express the horror I experienced during those two months, or what I still feel when memory reverts to the scene."

Is it true that a guy was sentenced to death because he ate most of the Democrats in a county out west?

You're thinking of Alferd Packer, and much of the story is a popular myth. Here's the true story: In 1873, Alferd Packer and five other residents of Colorado went prospecting. They got lost in a snowstorm and their provisions ran out. When authorities came upon the scene months later, the five others had been killed, and one of them had been partially roasted and eaten. Packer was convicted of murder and cannibalism.

That part is true. Now, here's where the legend kicks in: At the end of Packer's trial, the judge supposedly exclaimed, "Stand up, you man-eating son of a bitch, and receive your sentence. There were seven Democrats in Hinsdale County, but you, you voracious, man-eating son of a bitch, you ate five of them. I sentence you to be hanged by the neck until you're dead, dead, dead, as a warning against reducing the Democratic population of the state."

Back to reality now. Packer served seventeen years and lived out the rest of his life as a semirecluse (and, some say, a vegetarian), spending some of his time hanging around the *Denver Post* building as an unofficial security guard (this may have been out of gratitude since a *Denver Post* reporter had been responsible for getting his sentence reduced). Incidentally, a century later, the students at Boulder University voted to name the school cafeteria the "Alferd Packer Memorial Grill." Its most popular menu item has been the El Canibal Burrito.

What's the name of the musical based on Alferd Packer?

Cannibal! The Musical. It's a loose (and we mean very loose) interpretation of the real events. It was

Where can I find information on the Alferd Packer Trail Run challenge?

written by the creator of the irreverent, foul-mouthed but much adored, cartoon *South Park*.

INJUN TROUBLES

I can't believe that L. Frank Baum wrote that Indians should all be exterminated. What was that about?

The kindly author of *The Wizard of Oz* wrote two editorials on the subject when he was editor of the *Aberdeen Saturday Pioneer*. Here is the core of one of them: *"The Pioneer has before declared that our only safety depends upon the total extermination of the Indians. Having wronged them for centuries we had better, in order to protect our civilization, follow it up by one more wrong and wipe these untamed and untamable creatures from the face of the earth. In this lies safety for our settlers and the soldiers who are under incompetent commands. Otherwise, we may expect future years to be as full of trouble with the redskins as those have been in the past."*

Baum ended this editorial with a quote in which he apparently completely missed the ironic semantical point of the original speaker: "An eastern contemporary, with a grain of wisdom in its wit, says that 'when the whites win a fight, it is a victory, and when the Indians win it, it is a massacre.' "

What's sad and scary is that what he wrote was not that far off from what was considered mainstream thought of the time. And in fact, the policy he outlined was pretty close to what became official national policy under Andrew Jackson. Jackson, it should be noted, won his fame as an army commander after making a killing (both financially and literally) by laying personal claim to lands after chasing off and killing the Indian people who lived there. It became the official policy to break treaties, steal land, and massacre entire villages of Native Americans, no matter what their age. Whether this excuses Baum or makes him all the more culpable is a question for the ethicists.

Who is Chivington, Colorado, named after?

Colonel John Chivington of the U.S. Army. As commander of the local fort, it was Chivington whom the delegation of Indians came to, trying to arrange a peace treaty. Carrying an American flag, 28 men and 105 women and children believed that they had reached a sympathetic ear. They were wrong. While the tribe went home and celebrated the peace they thought they'd achieved, Chivington gave a speech to his officers: "Damn any man who sympathizes with Indians! I have come to kill Indians, and believe it is right and honorable to use any means under God's heaven to kill Indians." That night, six hundred soldiers sneaked up on the Indian camp, where they raped, killed, and mutilated every person there. According to witnesses who came upon the scene the next day, every Indian was scalped and mutilated horribly. Men were castrated and woman had their genitals cut out. The soldiers paraded with their grisly souvenirs on impaled sticks and on their hats while the white citizens cheered. Chivington justified killing Indian babies in this case, as he had done many times before, because "Nits make lice!"

The United States government later launched investigations, but neither Chivington nor any of his men were charged with any crimes. And not long after, local citizens named the town in his honor.

Why did Indians scalp their victims?

Contrary to popular myth, it was *not* a Native American custom but a colonial one first. Scalping on the American continent was first instituted by the Dutch colonial government around New York when they actually set a bounty for killing Indians. They came up with the idea of requiring a scalp as concrete evidence of a kill before paying a claim. Other colonial governments thought this was a great idea, and the English and French began using the same system to tally kills. Eventually, even the Native Americans picked it up for their own internal bookkeeping.

How dangerous were the Indians to wagon trains crossing the plains?

You'd think from the movies that they were a constant threat. In reality, during the time between 1840 and 1860—when many of the worst hostilities took place—your chances of dying of sickness on the wagon trains was much higher than dying from a Native American attack. During those two decades, about 250,000 whites and African Americans traveled across the plains. Of those, 362 died in battles with Indians; during the same battles, 426 Indians died.

What was the Trail of Tears?

The Trail of Tears was the name given to a series of forced marches in the 1830s, moving five Indian tribes from the woods and fields of their southeastern homelands to a desert wasteland, which was officially designated as "Indian Country." Although promised "conveyances and provisions" to get them across the 800 miles to the new lands, the "conveyances" turned out to be their own feet. About a quarter of the people died along the way, mostly children and the elderly. These were not warlike tribes, but actually were called "the Five Civilized Tribes" because they strove to coexist with settler society—they farmed and ranched, built roads, schools, and churches, developed a written language, and even attempted to fight removal by appealing to the Supreme Court. However, their lands were too valuable, and American racism was too ingrained to let them live in peaceful coexistence.

Later, even most of the desert wasteland was stolen by the whites, and nowadays, Indian Country is now called by a newer name, "the State of Oklahoma."

CUSTER'S REVENGE

Did anyone survive Custer's last stand?

Quite a few did. All of them were Native Americans, however.

There was one survivor from Custer's party, an Indian translator. However, the American government got its revenge—they used his defeat as an excuse to indiscriminately wipe out tribes in the area.

How did Crazy Horse die?

When he left the Indian reservation without permission to take his wife to see her parents, he was arrested by U.S. soldiers. When he realized the soldiers were going to lock him up in a guardhouse, he struggled against the officers holding his arms. A soldier then ran him through with a bayonet.

"O, had I but followed the arts!" wailed a character in Shakespeare's <u>Twelfth Night.</u> He was bemoaning the time he'd wasted pursuing "fencing, dancing, and bear-baiting," and other pop-culture diversions of the day. And so should we. So turn off the TV and join us in embracing the more enlightening aspects of life.

AH, THE SIMPLE LIFE

How long did Henry David Thoreau live as a hermit when writing **Walden?**

Believe it or not, some argue Thoreau never really lived out in the "wilds" at all. As proof, they say that at no time did he ever reside more than two miles from his mother and sister's house in Concord. Thoreau's house was situated so that he could see the bustling Concord-Lincoln highway across his lot, and the Fitchburg railroad tracks whooshed by on the other side of Walden Pond. He would often go for suppers and beg cookies from his mother on daily trips into the bustling city.

Even at home, he was rarely alone for long. His little cabin easily fit a dozen visitors and often did. His regular guests included Ralph Waldo Emerson and Nathaniel Hawthorne, and tourists often knocked on his door hoping to meet the "recluse."

BIPOLAR EXPLORER

How long did the writing of Dr. Jekyll and Mr. Hyde *take?*

I'm assuming you've heard amazing statistics on this or you wouldn't be asking. What you've heard is probably true, or close to it. Robert Louis Stevenson, reportedly suffering from tuberculosis and on a six-day cocaine binge, wrote the classic in a frenzy. His wife commented that it seemed unbelievable a man in his condition could've produced a work that long (60,000 words—only a little shorter than this tome in your hands) in six days.

STRONG ENOUGH FOR A MAN, INVENTED BY A WOMAN

Did men always perform all of the roles—male and female—in Japanese Kabuki theatre?

Although this was true in European theatre in Shakespeare's time, the reverse was true in Japan—at least in the beginning. Perhaps that was because the art form was invented by a woman. Kabuki first came about in the spring of 1603 in Kyoto. Women, led by a shrine maiden named Okuni, dressed up in elaborate costumes with heavy makeup and danced with exaggerated movements before the Kitani shrine, playing both male and female roles. The people loved this new art form, and it became very popular. In 1629, however, shogun Iemitsu decreed it immoral for women to dance in public and made Kabuki an all-male affair. Men and boys would don heavy makeup and play both male and female roles—not unlike Elizabethan era theatre. Not many years later, however, under another shogun, Ietsuna, boys were prohibited from participating in these dramatic productions, transforming the plays once more and making them an all-*adult* male venture. Even now, traditional Kabuki is still played by a male cast of characters. Men who specialize in women's roles are called *onnagata.*

I LOST MY TWAIN OF THOUGHT

Did Mark Twain say, "There are three kinds of lies: lies, damn lies, and statistics"?

Yes, he said it in his autobiography. But he didn't invent the phrase, he was simply borrowing it. The man responsible for the witticism (or truism, as the case may be) is Benjamin Disraeli, British author and politician. To his credit, Twain rightly attributes Disraeli in his book. To the discredit of authors since, they've disregarded his attribution and credited Twain himself.

AESOP LOVES ME, THIS I KNOW

Jeeves, can you point me to the Bible verse about God helping those who help themselves?

Nope, because it doesn't exist. It wasn't Moses, David, Peter, Paul, or Mary. Instead, it was that fable-telling fiend (who may or may not have really existed), Aesop. In Aesop's tale of "Hercules and the Wagoner," a man's wagon gets stuck in a muddy rut, not unlike muddy ruts we've all found ourselves in. The man begins cursing the horses and then realizes that's not helping, so he moves on to the rut. When he's through cursing the rut, he cries out to the gods to help him, at which time our favorite mythical hero, Hercules, appears and berates the man: "Put your shoulders to the wheels, my man. Goad on your bullocks and never more pray to me for help, until you have done your best to help yourself, or depend upon it you will henceforth pray in vain."

As is usual with all of dear Aesop's stories, there is a moral: "Self-help is the best help," or, as some translations have it, "The gods help them that help themselves."

WHO'S AFRAID OF THE BIG BAD GOAT?

Virginia Woolf doesn't look like a goat from pictures. Why was her childhood nickname "The Goat"?

You clearly didn't have older brothers when you were growing up. There are no specific references as to why the name, but it may have been because of her temperament. Regardless, the name itself was said to have been meant affectionately. It was a nickname that stuck with her for the rest of her life.

AND HE DIDN'T GET HIS SECURITY DEPOSIT BACK

I've heard that Picasso painted everything in sight. How much of this is true?

Some of it is, for sure. He didn't "paint everything in sight," but he was a prolific painter in many senses of the word: He produced over 15,000 paintings in his lifetime—working on three or more canvases a day—and he also painted on surfaces other than canvas. The story goes that while renting an apartment in Barcelona in 1900, the newly whitewashed walls were too great a temptation for him. He lavishly decorated them with paintings. His landlord was unimpressed and told him he must pay to have them repainted. Picasso snippily remarked later, after becoming successful, "He could have sold the whole wall for a fortune if he had only had the sense to leave it."

WORK LIKE THE DICKENS

What was Charles Dickens's profession before he was a writer?

His working career was a little eclectic, and it started when he was quite young. At the age of 12, his father was in debtors' prison, and Charles was removed from school by his parents and sent away to work in a shoe polish factory called Warren's Shoeblacking Factory and Warehouse. His experiences there would later become the inspiration for many of the scenes of his stories about orphaned children. Later, after his parents' finances were more steady and Charles had received a bit more schooling, he went to work as an office boy for a solicitor. When his father was finally released from debtors' prison, the older Dickens got a job at a newspaper where young Charles was able to see writers and reporters in action. Not long after, he decided this was his calling and managed to land a job as a reporter for the *Morning Chronicle*. His beat was the House of Commons. In 1836 his first work, *Sketches by Boz,* was published, and thus began his rise to fame as a popular author. Thereafter, he made his living as an author.

KAMA MY PLACE AND I'LL TRY TO SUTRA

Who wrote the Kama Sutra, *and why?*

Kamasutra means "guidebook" (sutra) to "sensual pleasure" (kama), and most historians believe the *Kama Sutra* was translated into Sanskrit by a fellow named Malianaga Vatsyayana somewhere between the third and fifth centuries A.D. Vatsyayana broke it down into an easy-to-digest step-by-step guidebook so that the basics could be followed and remembered by readers (it would, after all, ruin the romantic moment if lovers had to keep stopping and referring to a book). But no one knows who penned the original holy scriptures that Vatsyayana rewrote.

Little to nothing is known about the author, Vatsyayana. In the texts of his *Kama Sutra,* he has this to say about himself and his reason for writing the guidebook:

> *After reading and considering the works of Babhravya and other ancient authors, and thinking over the meaning of the rules given by them, this treatise was composed according to the precepts of the Holy Writ, for the benefit of the world, by Vatsyayana, while leading the life of a religious student at Benares, and wholly engaged in the contemplation of the Deity. This work is not to be used merely as an instrument for satisfying our desires. A person acquainted with the true principles of this science, who perseveres his Dharma (virtue or religious merit), his Artha (worldly wealth) and his Kama (pleasure or sensual gratification), and who has regard to the customs of the people, is sure to obtain the mastery over his senses. In short, an intelligent and knowing person*

attending to Dharma and Artha and also to Kama, without becoming the slave of his passions, will obtain success in everything that he may do.

ACHTUNG, GUENTHER! IT LOOKS LIKE PHILLY!

Who painted that famous picture of Washington crossing the Delaware?

Washington Crossing the Delaware was painted by Emanuel Leutze, a German-born painter, living at the time in Germany. The river you see in the picture is actually a stand in for the Delaware. It's the Rhine. It's sort of fitting, actually: When Washington crossed the icy Delaware in the cold of winter, he was on his way to fight German mercenaries that had been hired by the British.

LYRE, LYRE, ROME'S ON FIRE

Did Nero really fiddle while Rome burned?

Not literally; they didn't have fiddles or even violins in ancient Rome. They did, however, have lyres. Nero played and composed on one regularly. He didn't consider himself a mere politician but a richly talented artist and musician as well. When fire swept through Rome in 64 A.D., many believed Nero was behind the blaze as a way of clearing out land for a lavish palace he had designed for himself. Rumors began to flourish that, as the fires blazed, Nero used them as inspiration for his compositions and gleefully played music while the whole of Rome burnt to the ground. There's no evidence he did either of these things. However, he did get his land, and he built an incredible home for himself. Nero—not unlike other early Roman emperors—was reckless with public funds and indifferent to the citizens of Rome. In 68 A.D. he was proclaimed a public enemy by the Roman Senate for his ruthlessness and lack of concern about state matters. Nero committed suicide before he could be captured by the Roman guard. With his dying breath he declared, "What a great artist dies in me!"

FUHRER, MEIN GOTT TO THEE!

What's the translation of the title of Hitler's book Mein Kampf?

In English, the book is titled *My Struggle*.

BODY OF WORK

Where's Voltaire buried?

He isn't, exactly. Or at least not in a place where you'd want to go visit his gravesite. Voltaire (real name: François-Marie Arouet) made a lot of enemies in his life because of his brilliant satires and treatises, especially those that attacked the intolerance, corruption, and irrationality of the religious establishment. When he died in 1778 and could no longer defend himself, those enemies struck back. He was denied burial in church ground until the abbey in Champagne relented. In 1791, his remains were moved to a place of honor within the Pantheon in Paris.

However, in 1814 a group of right-wing religious extremists decided that burial was too good for someone who had so hurt their feelings in his lifetime, so they broke in one night, stole Voltaire's remains, and dumped them in a garbage heap somewhere. Their craven act wasn't discovered for more than fifty years, so while the memorial in the Pantheon remains, his sarcophagus is but an empty shell.

Before his burial, his heart and brain had been removed. While his brain disappeared after being auctioned off in the late 1800s, his heart is still in France's possession—last time they checked at least—in the Bibliotheque Nationale, hopefully under a decent lock and key.

FLOWERS BLOOM IN A BUREAUCRAT'S SOUL

What was Walt Whitman's "day job"?

Some things never change. Even after publishing *Leaves of Grass*, one of America's greatest poets couldn't survive on a poet's royalties. He worked as a low-level Washington bureaucrat, as a clerk in the Indian Department. He often saw his big boss,

Abraham Lincoln, walking up the streets of Washington, D.C. Whitman was a loyal employee; his poem "Oh Captain, My Captain" was written in mourning for Lincoln after his assassination.

DO IT YOURSELF

Did Ben Franklin really say, "Masturbation is the best policy"?

No, that was Mark Twain humorously claiming Ben Franklin said that. In Twain's speech on masturbation (which they don't teach much in schools for some reason), Twain also had Franklin saying, "Masturbation is the mother of invention."

Ben Franklin may not have left many letters behind regarding masturbation, but he did leave a lengthy note to a dear friend on marriage and, short of matrimony, how to choose a mistress. Truth be told, this letter that we found in *Weird History 101* by John R. Stephens may have been more than a little tongue-in-cheek, but you can judge for yourself:

> *A single Man has not nearly the Value he would have in that State of Union. He is an incomplete Animal. He resembles the odd Half of a Pair of Scissors.*
>
> *If you get a prudent, healthy wife, your Industry in your Profession, with her good Economy, will be a Fortune sufficient. But if you will not take this Counsel, and persist in thinking a Commerce with the Sex is inevitable, then I repeat my former Advice that in your Amours you should* prefer old Women to young ones. *This you call a Paradox, and demand my reasons. They are these:*
>
> 1. *Because they have more Knowledge of the world, and their Minds are better stored with Observations; their Conversation is more improving, and more lastingly agreeable.*
>
> 2. *Because when Women cease to be handsome, they study to be good. To maintain their Influence over Man, they supply the Diminution of Beauty by an Augmentation of Utility. They learn to do a thousand Services, small and great, and*

are the most tender and useful of all Friends when you are sick. Thus they continue amiable. And hence there is hardly such a thing to be found as an old Woman who is not a good Woman.

3. *Because there is no hazard of children, which irregularly produced may be attended with much inconvenience.*

4. *Because through more Experience they are more prudent and discreet in conducting an Intrigue to prevent Suspicion. The Commerce with them is therefore safer with regard to your reputation; and regard to theirs, if the Affair should happen to be known, considerate People might be inclined to excuse an old Woman, who would kindly take care of a young Man, form his manners by her good Councils, and prevent his ruining his Health and Fortune among mercenary Prostitutes.*

5. *Because in every Animal that walks upright, the Deficiency of the Fluids that fill the Muscles appears first in the highest Part. The Face first grows lank and wrinkled; then the Neck; then the Breast and Arms; the lower parts continuing to the last as plump as ever; so that covering all above with a Basket, and regarding only what is below the Girdle, it is impossible of two Women to know an old from a young one. And as in the Dark all Cats are gray, the Pleasure of Corporal Enjoyment with an old Woman is at least equal and frequently superior; every Knack being by Practice capable by improvement.*

6. *Because the sin is less. The Debauching of a Virgin may be her Ruin, and make her for Life unhappy.*

7. *Because the Compunction is less. The having made a young Girl* miserable *may give you frequent bitter Reflections none which can attend making an old Woman* happy.

8th & lastly. *They are so grateful!!!*

Thus much for my Paradox. But still I advise you to marry immediately; being sincerely Your Affectionate Friend, Benj. Franklin

MARTIAL ARTS IMITATES ART

Did the artist (and the Teenage Mutant Ninja Turtle) Raphael have a last name or was he like Madonna and Prince?

He did. He was named at birth Raffaello Sanzio. Because the turtle creature was named for the Renaissance artist, we can assume he shares the same last name, as well.

Why is the Teenage Mutant Ninja Turtle, Michaelangelo, spelled differently from the artist Michelangelo?

The cartoon's artists, Kevin Eastman and Peter Laird, say it was a mistake. When they created the comic book series, computer spellcheckers weren't widely available. The turtle ended up with an extra "a" in his name purely by accident. It should be noted that both Laird and Eastman had been students of art history.

YEAH, YEAH, TELL ME ANOTHER ONE

Were the **Arabian Nights** *stories really told to save a king's young wife from execution?*

Possibly, but doubtful. The first story in the *Arabian Nights* anthology goes something like this: King Shahriya had been burned by the unfaithfulness of his first wife and had her killed. He vowed to never trust women again, so he would marry then execute his young brides on the morning after their honeymoon. He did this time and again and one day decided to marry his niece, Scheherazade. But she was quick on her toes and figured a way to prolong her life. On her wedding night, she asked the King if she could read her little sister a bedtime story. He agreed, so she told the best story she could concoct but saved the ending for the next night. The King, liking a good story as well as the next fellow, kept her alive an extra day to hear the ending to her story. But tricky as Scheherazade was, she started a *new* story for her sister the next night, leaving her audience hanging once again. She did this for a thousand nights—long enough for King Shahriya to fall in love with her and spare her life forever. The stories in the *Arabian Nights* tome are supposed to be Scheherazade's thousand stories that she told to save her own life.

It's a brilliant storytelling structure and one that had been used in India, where most literary historians believe this tale originated, since storytelling began. As a matter of fact, as real as the characters of Scheherazade and Shahriya may seem, the idea of creating a digest of short stories, all rolled up into one all-encompassing tale, was the norm at the time this story was first being told.

Historians believe that the stories within were collected from China, India, Egypt, Persia, and Arabia. The Arabian and Persian stories were passed down orally from generation to generation by professional storytellers who performed lavish plays and puppet shows in coffee houses all across the Middle East. It wasn't until about 1300 A.D. that these stories began to be written down. The translations we have today come from an Arabic tome that dates to about 1500.

Not everyone in the stories was completely fictitious, however. There was one known character in several of the stories in *Arabian Nights* who was real. His name was Caliph Harun al-Rashid—the character who in various tales was often found roaming the streets in disguise. He actually was ruler of the Muslim empire from about 786 A.D. and was much loved by his people.

ALL THAT JAZZ

During what years did the Harlem Renaissance take place?

Some accounts say from about 1925 to 1935, but the movement had actually begun many years before it was discovered by the rest of the world. During this decade following World War I, Rhodes scholar Alain Locke defined the movement of cultural enlightenment and African American pride within the district of Harlem, which then spread out to both black and white communities. Great names in literature such as Langston Hughes, Jean Toomer, Jessie Fauset, and Zora Neale Hurston emerged during this era, along with jazz greats like Jelly Roll Morton, Louis Armstrong, Duke Ellington, Ethel Waters, Josephine Baker, and Bessie Smith.

LIVE AND LET FLY

Who wrote Chitty Chitty Bang Bang?

Ian Fleming wrote the book. You may know him better by his other writings, however. He was the author who introduced the world to Bond. James Bond.

COMPOSING & DECOMPOSING

Did composer Salieri really try to swindle Mozart out of the Requiem, *like in the movie* Amadeus?

No. As the screenwriter Peter Shaffer puts it, "It's a fantasia based on fact. It is *not* a screen biography of Mozart and was never intended to be." Antonio Salieri was a contemporary of Mozart and admired his work very much. However well they knew each other, Mozart did not become dependent on him, and Salieri wasn't at Mozart's deathbed.

The *Requiem* was actually written for Count von Walsegg zu Stuppach, a rich amateur musician. The count liked to throw lavish parties and play unsigned scores to see if his guests could guess the composer who had written it, oftentimes passing the works off as his own. An employee of the count's, Anton Herzog, recounted these scenes as such:

> The secretly organized scores he generally copied out in his own hand, and presented them for the parts to be copied out. We never saw an original score. The quartets were then played, and we had to guess who the composer was. Usually we suggested it was the Count himself, because from time to time he actually composed some small things; he smiled and was pleased that we (as he thought) had been mystified; but we were amused that he took us for such simpletons. We were all young and thought this an innocent pleasure which we gave our lord. And in such fashion the mystifications continued among us for some years.

The count also requested that the piece be such that it could be played at his recently deceased wife's memorial as well—killing two birds with one stone, as it were. When Mozart passed away, the *Requiem* was left partially unfinished with only two movements left, so Constanze, Mozart's wife, delivered the piece and was paid by Count von Walsegg. Furthermore, she asked Mozart's student Franz Süssmayer to finish the *Requiem* so she could publish it and get some royalties from her dead husband's piece. Süssmayer did his best to finish it in Mozart's style.

However, the film's portrayal of Mozart's delirium was somewhat accurate. He was dying during the writing of the *Requiem,* and he did suffer from high fever and hallucinations. At one point, he offhandedly commented that he felt he was writing his own *Requiem.* And in a way he was: The unfinished *Requiem* was performed, unbeknownst to the Count, at Mozart's memorial service.

Ask!

Where can I hear Mozart's *Requiem* online?

How many children did Mozart have? Were they musically inclined, too?

Wolfgang Amadeus Mozart and his wife, Constanze Weber, despite their money troubles, were a loving couple up until his early death at age 35. The playful pair kept Constanze in a perpetual state of pregnancy. They had a total of six children in their eight-and-a-half year marriage, only two of which survived: their second child, Karl Thomas, and their sixth child, Franz Xaver Wolfgang. Karl Thomas grew up to be an official on the staff of the viceroy of Naples. Franz Xaver inherited his father's interest in music and conducted extensively in Europe. However, Mozart was an impossible figure to measure up to. As George Bernard Shaw once noted: "[Jr. was] An amiable man, a clever musician, an excellent player, but hopelessly extinguished by his father's reputation. How could any man do what was expected from Mozart's son? Not Mozart himself even."

Was Beethoven always deaf? How could he play the piano?

Oh, no. It wasn't until his twenties that he began to lose his hearing in any significant way, and by that time he had already studied with the likes of Joseph Haydn and Mozart. He gave his first solo concert in his late twenties. However, by the time he reached his early thirties his hearing was gone, and he could no longer properly play the piano. At this point, he admitted to considering suicide because his personal loss was so overwhelming. To the benefit of classical music, he discovered he could, despite being deaf, still compose. He wrote symphonies and concertos for the remainder of his life, most of them being the best he'd ever written. Beethoven's overall accomplishments included writing scores of written music, extending the length of the piano concerto and symphony, and adding instruments to the orchestra, including the piccolo and the trombone. And what would an orchestra be without a trombone?

NICE PLAY, SHAKESPEARE

Was there a "real" Romeo and Juliet that the Shakespeare play was based on?

Some say yes, but after so many years and so many tellings and retellings, it's impossible to verify. What we do know is that Shakespeare based his play on an old Italian tale that was possibly based on real events. The folktale dates back to sometime around 1500 but was first transcribed in 1530 by Luiga da Porta in a story called *Giulietta e Romeo.* Da Porta's contribution to the folktale was giving last names to the famous lovers. The names he gave the rival houses, the Capulets and Montagues, were names of real Italian families that he lifted directly from Dante's writings in *Purgatorio VI.*

After da Porta pinned down the characters, names, places, and plot, the story was retold in *Romeo e Giulietta,* an Italian novella by Matteo Bandello in 1554, and then again in a French novella in 1559 by Pierre Boaistuau. Poet Arthur Brooke wrote a poem based on the novella titled "Romeus & Juliet," and it was this that was the basis for Shakespeare's play.

Shakespeare adjusted the story in some ways. The poem had the lovers' story unfold over three months; Shakespeare had it unfold over an implausibly quick five-day period. Shakespeare also, to make it work as a play, added depth to the characters. Previous versions of the story were more sketchy and one-dimensional. But his most important change was altering Juliet's age from 18 to 13. This may have come from the idea in Elizabethan England that Italian girls matured faster than other women. Or Shakespeare may have been making a point about young love. Or perhaps the boy who was scheduled to play Juliet looked too young to be plausible as an eighteen-year-old. Whatever the case, his contributions to this tale have stood the test of time. There is no retelling that doesn't rely on the basic elements of his classic play.

Ask! Where can I find the play King Lear online?

Did Shakespeare smoke?

He definitely smoked some tobacco in a pipe, as did most men in 16th-century Elizabethan England. And recent excavations of his Stratford-upon-Avon home have uncovered that he may have smoked a little more than tobacco. Residues in pipes found there contained trace amounts of cocaine and marijuana. However, what this means is hotly debated, as there are no records that cocaine was used at all in England before about 200 years ago. And although *Cannabis sativa* was used for clothing, paper, rope, and other products, in England during this time period there seems to be no other indication that it was used as a drug or medicine. Still, other experts point to Shakespeare's own writings as proof that he wasn't foreign to mind-altering substances. Take his Sonnet 76. It's part of a short ditty to a lover lamenting the fact that he's run out of original ways to express himself:

> *Why is my verse so barren of new pride,*
> *So far from variation or quick change?*
> *Why, with the time do I not glance aside*
> *To new-found methods and to compounds strange?*
> *Why write I still all one, ever the same,*
> *And keep invention in a noted weed,*
> *That every word doth almost tell my name,*
> *Showing their birth and where they did proceed?*

The term "noted weed" aside; "compounds strange" is said by some scholars to be a known reference to drugs. More evidence is surely needed in this case. Stay tuned.

Ask! Are there any accurate portraits of Shakespeare?

LIVING BY THE SWORD

What if they threw a war and nobody came? Like a car with-out an engine, war couldn't be won or lost unless there were those willing to do the fighting. From pilots and their airplanes to the Hatfields and the McCoys, we seem to be fascinated with the warriors throughout history.

CURSE YOU, RED BARON!

Snoopy never got him, but did anybody ever shoot down the Red Baron?

Manfred von Richthofen was credited with shooting down 80 aircraft during World War I. However, skill and luck finally failed the 25-year-old pilot in 1918. While dogfighting with a Canadian pilot over Allied territory, the Red Baron was fatally hit by Australian gunners on the ground below. The Australians respectfully buried his body with full military honors.

Was the Red Baron really a baron?

No. In his native Germany he was called *Der Rote Kampffliegger,* meaning "The Red Battle Flyer." Why the "Red"? Before effective anti-aircraft guns made camouflage a necessity, World War I pilots tended to paint their planes bright colors as a way of identifying each other. Von Richthofen favored red. These colorful planes looked so brightly festive when grouped together that earthbound soldiers called them "the flying circus."

Ask! Where can I find a collection of Snoopy's battles against the Red Baron?

SHAKEN, NOT STIRRED

Why is a gasoline bomb called a "Molotov cocktail"?

There are a couple of theories of origin, but the Molotov name probably comes from Stalin's premier and foreign minister, Vyacheslav Mikhailovich Molotov. It was while he was minister of defense that Russians started the policy of using petrol bombs as an anti-tank weapon so that in any situation, they would have some sort of defense, even if ammunition were low. However, it must be noted that Molotov's original surname was Scriabin. Just as Stalin adopted a name for its meaning, Scriabin chose Molotov, the Russian word for hammer, to be his new last name. So it could be that the gasoline bomb got its name from the tool and not the man. Regardless of how the Molotov cocktail got its name, the double meaning has a certain explosive impact.

Ask! Who was the first to use exploding bombs?

MOUNT'N CASUALTIES

How many people were killed in the war between the Hatfields and the McCoys?

Thirteen killed, eight jailed, one hanged.

What started the Hatfield–McCoy Feud?

There was already a great deal of tension between the two families about big issues and small, including some conflicting loyalties in America's Civil War. It came to a head after a McCoy accused a Hatfield of stealing one of his razorback hogs. It was yet another war started by a pig (see page 78).

Is it true that a marriage ended the Hatfield–McCoy feud?

That's a really heartwarming ending to the story, but a complete myth, nonetheless. True, there had been a Romeo-&-Juliet–style romance between two of the young-uns, but their romance lasted only long enough to start a pregnancy before the fickle young Hatfield boy took up with his girlfriend's cousin and wisely moved out of the feuding zone before the fireworks really started. Nothing really ended the feud, exactly; it just sort of trickled out as the families dwindled and the law intervened.

ATOM AND EVIL

How many people were killed when the United States dropped nuclear bombs on Japan?

An exact figure is hard to pin down, but more than a third of a million.

Who were Little Boy and Fat Man?

The atomic bombs that destroyed Hiroshima and Nagasaki.

How many nuclear explosions have been set off since 1945?

More than 1,800. About half by the United States.

MANY HAPPY RETURNS

How could the Australian aborigines get their boomerangs to return to them if they actually hit something while hunting?

They didn't. As you would suspect, if a returning boomerang actually makes contact with something, its flight is cut short and it won't return to the thrower. Here's a quick primer on boomerangs: Boomerangs are simply a curved version of the old throwing sticks that have been around for about fifteen thousand years in various ancient cultures. The Hopi Indians of North America used them to hunt rabbit; the ancient Egyptians and Australian natives hunted and fought wars with them. The returning boomerang—the type you and I are most familiar with—was specially invented by Australian aborigines. It is believed by some experts that the device was used to scare birds out of their nests and into the hunters' nets; however, most believe it may have simply been a sophisticated toy. Today, boomerangs are *only* used as toys or sport devices around which there have developed some quite sophisticated clubs and tournaments.

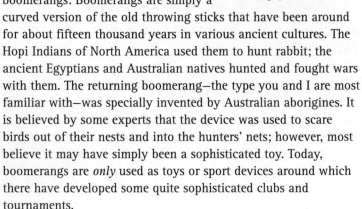

Ask! How do I make a boomerang come back?

ROME WASN'T DESTROYED IN A DAY

Where does the word "arena" come from?

It was passed down to us from the ancient Romans. To sop up the endlessly flowing blood, the staging area of an ancient Roman arena was made of wood but covered with sand. "Sand" is *harena* in Latin, from which the word "arena" was spawned. Underneath the wood and *harena* was a dark, noisy labyrinth filled with the stench and noise of prisoners, gladiators, and wild animals, who could "magically" enter the arena by way of a series of trapdoors.

What was a typical day of entertainment at the Roman Colosseum?

Blood sports became so popular in Rome that the Colosseum was built specially for that purpose. The Colosseum had seating for about 50,000 people. The ringside seats were reserved for the emperor, senators, and other bigwigs. People of progressively lower status sat farther away, proportionate to their rank. (Women and foreigners were seated in the top rows.)

The morning act was gladiator games. They began with the combatants parading into the arena, led by the sponsor of the games (in Latin—authors beware—he was called the *editor*). In Rome, this was usually the emperor; in outlying areas it was usually a high-ranking magistrate. Music accompanied the procession and the subsequent bouts of combat.

The first events might be mock fights with wooden weapons, which were often followed by the animal acts. Sometimes these animals were trained to perform tricks, but more often they were there merely to be killed—the more common animals first, then progressively they presented the more exotic, sometimes in combat against each other, sometimes killed by an animal fighter called a *bestiarii*.

In the stands, people could pass any slow parts of the day by frequenting the food merchants, bookmakers, and prostitutes offering their specialties. But the lunch break was not a time to wander far because that's when the state executed criminals who had committed particularly serious crimes, like murder, arson, sacrilege, and treason. (It was on the latter two charges that Christians were most often convicted, for refusing to acknowledge the Roman gods and the divinity of the emperor.) The hope then, as now, was that executions would act as a deterrent. (And then, as now, capital punishment *wasn't* especially effective, as demonstrated by the fact that the Christians thrived and eventually took over Rome.) One form of execution was throwing the condemned person to wild animals; another was forcing them into dramatic reenactments of bloody myths or battles; still another was placing them into battle after battle until killed. (Refusing to participate was not a viable option: If they didn't show enough enthusiasm for battle, they were prodded with hot pokers from ringside guards.)

After lunch came the mortal combat of the gladiators. Although it is popularly believed that the bouts began with gladiators chanting to the emperor, "We who are about to die salute you," historians say that there's little evidence that this was a part of the customary ceremony.

Gladiators would fight one-on-one or on teams. If one was injured, disarmed, or otherwise willing to concede defeat, he held up his left index finger; spectators signaled with hand gestures whether they wanted the losing fighter spared or put to death. (Despite common belief, the signals were not "thumbs down" for death and "thumbs up" for mercy. Historians say that "thumbs up" voted for death, and a fist or waved handkerchief for a reprieve.) The *editor* made the final decision, usually following the disposition of the crowd. If the gladiator was to be killed, he was expected to accept the killing blow without flinching or crying out. Some historians believe that there was also a ritual for checking the fallen gladiator for any signs of life, administering another fatal blow if necessary, and dragging the body offstage with a hook through a gate called the *Porta Libitinensis* in honor of Libitina, the death goddess.

The largest gladiator contest, given as a victory celebration by the emperor Domitian in 90 A.D., featured 5,000 contestants and resulted in the death of 2,000 humans and 250 animals. Most, though, were much more modest than that—in fact, after Julius Caesar presented an exhibition of 300 gladiator battles in one glorious event, the Roman Senate voted to place limits on the number of contestants per event.

Were all gladiators either slaves or prisoners?

Well, think of the job description: "Fight and be killed for the amusement of others." Consider the oath when you signed up where you agreed to be "burned with fire, shackled with chains, whipped with rods and killed with steel." Would you choose to apply for a job like this? To be fair, there were a few perks. You were treated and fed fairly well in gladiator school. You might survive for a few battles and be showered with prize money, gifts, fame, and adulation. ("Thrax is the heart throb of all the girls," read graffiti found on Pompeii's gladiator arena.) Finally, there was the infinitesimal chance that you'd survive enough bouts to be released from being a gladiator and go back to your life as a slave or freeman, or become a nobleman's bodyguard or an instructor in a gladiator school.

So, yes, the vast majority of gladiators were slaves, condemned criminals, and prisoners of war, but not quite all. Some desperate and bankrupt freemen, jumping at the hiring fee, glory, and any prize money they might manage to win, joined the ranks for an agreed-upon term of service. Some survived long enough to go free again.

And finally, there were the dilettantes and novelty-act gladiators. These wanna-be noblemen included the insane emperor Commodus, who wanted to display valor by jumping into the ring with real gladiators. They usually survived their "battles" by virtue of the fact that they were supplied with real swords while their opponents were given dull weapons . . . or none at all. (Commodus himself eventually paid for his macho displays when he was deliberately strangled by an assassin during what was supposed to have been a fixed wrestling match.) The novelty gladiators—dwarfs and women were both quite popular— also had less of a risk of being forced to die in their battles because they were there more as a diversion for the blood-jaded crowd.

> **Which emperor was the one depicted in the movie Gladiator?**
> Commodus.

Did gladiators who fought against animals use the same weapons as those who fought against other gladiators?

Actually, it was a matter of honor that the animal fighters, called *bestiarii,* were considered below true gladiators in rank. However, neither is to be confused with the condemned criminals, who were thrown defenseless into the midst of hungry animals to be torn to pieces for sport. Actually, a *bestiarum* had a relatively cushy job; he often "hunted" animals from the safety of the spectator seating area or entered the ring accompanied by hounds. Their weapons were bows, spears, and sometimes daggers, and they killed wild and exotic animals in huge abundance. For example, 5,000 animals were killed on the first day the Colosseum opened in 80 A.D. A vast industry supplied exotics from all over the Roman Empire; the first giraffe ever seen in Rome was butchered there. (It had been expected to put up a good fight because the Romans thought it was a vicious cross between a leopard and a camel, but the harmless herbivore was quickly slaughtered, to the cheers of the good citizens.) Some species were rendered extinct by the "sport," including the North African elephant.

Unlike the *bestiarii*, gladiators were in direct danger and faced terrible odds. Some were strong enough to survive for several battles and lucky enough to fight only a few fights a year. As characters in a perverse fantasy game, each gladiator was assigned to a class of warrior and given specific weapons that matched the category. For example, a *mirmillo*, dressed in fish designs and armed with a sword and shield, might fight against a *retiarium*, armed with a fishing net and trident. For comic relief (to all but the combatants), some gladiators fought as *andabatae*, wearing helmets without eyeholes (so that they flailed wildly like kids with a piñata), hoping to hit each other. Other gladiators fought with two swords and no shield; or on horseback; or from chariots; or with lassos; or clad in the armor and weapons of Rome's enemies, past and present.

Why would the Romans think that blood and death was a good spectator sport?

We aren't that far removed from them, alas. Look at our own sports; look at our movies and TV shows; listen to rap lyrics. At least the Romans claimed that they had a higher purpose in their blood lust. They thought that seeing death would train their population to be

> **What did some gladiators eat in the hope that it would repel lions?**
> Onions.

good warriors. Furthermore, the blood sports had religious significance. They had begun as a component of funeral ceremonies, based on the idea that shedding human blood somehow helped the soul of the departed move along to the next world.

Didn't gladiators rebel once and nearly take over Italy?

That would be Spartacus and his gang. A deserter from the Roman army, Spartacus was sold as a slave and trained as a gladiator. He escaped in 73 B.C. and gathered an army of 70,000 runaway slaves on Mount Vesuvius. They defeated five Roman armies and escaped to Cisalpine Gaul, where Spartacus intended to disband his armies and send them to their homes. Instead, they thought it over and decided to stay in Italy and plunder the villages. After two years, Spartacus was killed in battle, the insurrection ground to a halt, and a multitude of captured rebels were crucified as an example to us all.

Did the gladiola get its name from "gladiator"?

No, but both the warrior and the plant got their names from *gladius,* Latin for "sword." If you look at a gladiola and squint your eyes a bit, you can sort of see that the leaves surrounding the flower stalk look like green swords. And no, the radiator didn't get its name from "gladiator," either.

Ask! What did the ancient Greeks wear into battle?

YOU SUNK MY BATTLESHIP!

When was the first submarine used in battle?

During the Civil War, the *H. L. Hunley* (named after its financier, Horace Hunley) was (sort of) successfully used in battle. Although it sank the Union's *Housatonic* in shallow water by ramming bombs up against the sides of the battleship, in the process it sank itself as well. Five lives were lost on the Union side during the incident; however, the Confederate's *Hunley* lost its entire crew.

During the same time period, the Russians put an orchestra in a submarine, sent it down, and played a rendition of the Russian national anthem for an emperor's coronation. When the band played underwater, the song could be heard by ships all around the harbor. In contrast to America's submarine experience, no one was killed during this mission, and the orchestra bravely came up with the ship.

GREENBACKS, GREYBACKS & GOOBERS

Where did the slang term "greenbacks" come from?

This slang word for Union money came from the mouths of American Civil War soldiers—or, as they called each other, *graybacks* and *yankees*. A slue of slang terms originated from these guys, many of them still in use today. Take for instance *breadbasket* (stomach), *Chief cook and bottle washer* (someone in charge who can multitask well), *fit to be tied* (madder'n a hornet!), *horse sense* (common sense), *snug as a bug* (very comfortable), *skedaddle* (run along), *blowhard* (someone who boasts), *fit as a fiddle* (healthy and in shape), *uppity* (conceited), *goobers* (peanuts), and *hunkey dorey* (good).

Other terms originating during the Civil War, either lost to us now or completely changed in meaning over the years, were *sawbones* (surgeon), *possum* (a buddy), *bully!* (hurray!), *screamers* or *quickstep* (diarrhea), and *buggar* (an officer).

> **What Civil War song hit the charts in the 1950s?**
> "Love Me Tender," by Elvis Presley.

A COUPLE OF REAL BOOBS

Were the Amazons real? Did they really burn off their breasts?

There is evidence that nomadic tribes of warrior women existed in Asia Minor, as Greek accounts have suggested, but it's clear that not everything in these tales was based in fact. In tombs unearthed in the region (and other regions, it might be noted) both men and women were buried with weapons. This suggested that men and women most likely fought alongside one another. One burial site in particular has given archaeologists reason to believe that many of these steppe tribes had women warriors. A young girl of about 14 was buried with weapons and armor, and she also had bowed legs, strongly suggesting that she had been raised to ride on horseback, as most warriors of this time period were.

As to the issue of breasts, some of the Greek stories tell of ferocious warrior women burning off one of their breasts, and other stories do not. In terms of the archaeological finds, there's been no evidence of this practice.

Some experts believe the "Amazon women" myth came from the ancient Greek encounters with the Hittites, a civilization that worshipped goddesses and used priestesses. At the time of the Greek writings, Hittite men wore their hair long and paid homage to female images in their religion. It's possible that there was a gender-confusion problem—that the lonely Greek soldiers saw the Hittite guys and thought they were gals. Because Hittite remains are not as exciting as ancient Greek remains, it's a culture that hasn't been studied as much as it should. But therein may lie the answer to the Amazon question.

Ask!

Where can I find out about cultures that have used women warriors?

SO HELL IS JUST LIKE OSLO, THEN

What was the name of heaven to the ancient Norse people?

The Norse heaven for slain warriors was called Valhalla, meaning, literally, "hall of the slain." In Old Norse mythology, brave warriors killed in battle were brought to Valhalla by Valkyries, special death maidens. During an average day in the afterlife, dead warriors fought battles, and their wounds from a hard day of fighting were miraculously healed before nightfall when they dined with Odin, the king of the gods. Here the warriors would wait until Ragnarök, the day of the last battle of the world. At this point, it was promised that all of the old gods would fall away and a new era of love and peace would rise from the ashes. In contrast, regular Norse people—those dishonored by dying of old age or disease—were taken to a goddess named Hel. She resided in a place called "Underearth," which was devoid of joy and happiness, torture or pain. Underearth was sort of a neutral, ho-hum afterlife. It was this Scandinavian Hel, the goddess of the netherworld, that gave Christians the name for their infinitely more miserable afterlife locale, Hell.

Where does the old cry "hurrah!" come from? What does it mean?

It's from an old Norse warrior word "Huzzah!" which meant "On to paradise!"

YOU WIN THE BATTLE? NO, ZULUS!

I've heard that Zulu warriors armed only with spears held off colonial troops from taking parts of West Africa. How could that be?

The Zulu defeated the British in the Battle of Isandhlwana in 1879 by outgeneraling them, so to speak. In other words, they had an intricate plan, drawing the British closer and closer while they quietly surrounded them. They then sent waves of warriors rushing straight into the British lines, heedless of British guns, cannons, and death until they were on top of them. The Zulu warriors killed almost a thousand British soldiers before the colonial army even knew what had happened.

For years, the British blamed the loss in this war on a lack of planning and implementation, but in reality, the British fought all of the other small African kingdoms the same way in their effort to force them into accepting British rule. The Zulu, under the chief Cetshwayo, were simply better soldiers and better strategists.

The British unfortunately learned from this experience that the only way to win against the Zulu was to totally annihilate them, preferably from a distance. The Zulu soldiers continued to give the British army a run for their money; however, the British "took no prisoners," literally, in the next battle later that year. Ruthlessness and superior weaponry won in the end, and the Brits eventually defeated the tribesmen.

What is the war dance of the Zulu warriors?

The Zulu perform an intricate ritual before going to battle: The regiment, which is up to 1,000 warriors, congregate in the cattle kraal (the area blocked off for cattle near or within the village area) and jump around, miming their moves in battle. This is done in full war regalia, which can include headdresses of animal skins, and/or ostrich feathers; civet skins rolled and sewed into a skirt that looks like its made of monkey tails; and cow tails hung around the neck, arms, and legs. They sing unique regiment songs, getting psyched up to do battle.

SAY THERE, SOLDIER, HAVE YOU ANY GREY POUPON?

How long did the Rough Riders exist as a fighting force?

Not long at all, except in American legend. Teddy Roosevelt, anxious for a war with Spain, resigned as Secretary of the Navy and was authorized to put together a thousand-man volunteer cavalry force. Roosevelt was a Harvard boy, and so most of his early recruits were of similar ivy-league backgrounds. Figuring cavalry members should know something about horses, he favored steeple chasers and polo players from the plains of Cambridge, Princeton, and private clubs up and down the eastern seaboard. (In his memoirs, he recounted a bull session that took place on the troop freighter to Cuba in which a spirited discussion of Aryan root-words broke down into a melee "as to how far Balzac could be said to be the founder of the modern realistic school of fiction.")

Roosevelt began realizing that "Rough Riders" was going to end up an ironic nomenclature if he didn't round out his forces with something more than polo-playing boola-boola boys named Bucky, Dudley, and Guy. He began recruiting from the American frontier and added in a ragtag mix of cowboys, Indians, and Indian-fighters.

After some quick drilling and training, the boys were sent off on ships to the beaches of Cuba. The only problem was that most of their horses and burros were left behind on the dock in Florida. The few animals that made it onto the boat became disoriented after being dropped into the Cuban surf. After swimming madly from boat to boat instead of toward land, most of them drowned (as did two human Rough Riders). So, when the cavalry force braved Spanish gunfire capturing San Juan Hill, the Buckys and buckaroos of the Rough Riders were mounted on nothing more than their own shoe leather.

The Spanish, outnumbered 14 to one, put up a brief resistance before retreating, leaving their still-warm dinners for the conquering Americans to eat. Some Rough Riders died from bullets and artillery during their one day of active warfare, and more died when yellow fever invaded their camp weeks later. Still, the campaign was dramatized as a glorious triumph by the bored newspapermen who had been hanging around Havana drinking and waiting for a war to start.

Teddy Roosevelt came back home a war hero and rode his fame into national office. Following their one and only shot at combat, the Rough Riders disbanded. The brave warriors—finally reunited with their horses—rode gloriously back to their cattle ranches, Indian reservations, and polo grounds to the loud "Huzzahs!" of a grateful nation.

Ask! Where can I see military uniforms?

IN THE ARMS OF AMERICA

When were the Buffalo Soldiers disbanded?

The Buffalo Soldiers were the ninth and tenth cavalries of the United States Army, which, in those segregated times, were made up entirely of African Americans. They were first formed in 1866 and sent to the West to fight Indians, protect settlers, capture outlaws, and patrol the border with Mexico. During the Spanish-American War, they rescued some of Teddy Roosevelt's Rough Riders in the Battle of San Juan Hill, and they fought bravely during World Wars I and II. It wasn't until the Korean War that the Army ended racial segregation in its ranks, and that's when the history of the Buffalo Soldiers officially ended.

How did the Buffalo Soldiers get their name?

Native Americans gave the troops the name, probably because they hadn't seen many African Americans and thought the soldiers' short, dark, curly hair resembled the mane of the buffalo. The name was thought to be a sign of respect because the buffalo was an important animal to the Indians.

Did women serve in the Buffalo Soldier regiment?

Not legally. However, there was a woman named Cathay Williams—a former slave from Independence, Missouri—who secretly served as soldier William Cathay for two years during the Civil War. When she fell ill in 1868, she was discovered and discharged. She later opened a boarding house in Raton, New Mexico, which was a frequent stopping point for General Phil Sheridan.

KNIGHT'S WORK, IF YOU CAN GET IT

Who would win: a guy with a battle-ax or a guy with a joust?

A battle-ax, certainly. Why? Because a joust isn't a weapon in and of itself; it's a specific type of competition at a medieval tournament. Two armored knights would mount horses and face one another, each holding a lance. They would then charge and see which knight could topple the other first. Although metal-tipped lances were sometimes used in battle by knights, they were primarily the stuff of entertainment at the tourney.

Let's assume for a moment you were asking about a lance versus a battle-ax. A lance was good at knocking over a horse-riding opponent, but not so good at driving him through or lopping off his head. It was too easy to lose the end of a lance to the chop of a sword, too. The battle-ax would most likely win this war.

Was a battle-ax different from a regular wood-chopping ax?

Indeed. The battle-ax had a shorter handle. When chopping wood, a long handle is necessary for a wide swing. In battle, and in dealing with flesh, a short blow yields more accuracy and damage.

What was the weapon of choice for battle during the medieval times?

From the 13th to the 16th centuries, the long bow (a bow longer than the four-foot regular bow) was the official weapon of the British army. It could fire off 10 to 12 arrows a minute and was almost as powerful as the crossbow. Be assured, it won many a war during those days and was viewed in much the same way we view machine guns for military battle.

Of course, if you were an average foot soldier or a knight, you relied on the weapons that produced the hardest and most damaging blow but weren't too heavy or difficult to wield. This meant a sword was usually your best bet, and a two-handed sword was your weapon of choice. They could not only cut through chain mail but could also serrate the ends off pikes and axes. Other hand-held weapons included regular bows, spears, axes, daggers, flails, and maces, not to mention poles and pikes.

For demolishing structures, catapults, battering rams, trebuchets (those slinging machines), and ballistas (giant crossbows) were the ticket.

MADE IN JAPAN

What's the difference between a samurai and a Ninja warrior?

A samurai is a warrior, protector, and leader. A Ninja is someone who practices ninjutsu. Ninjutsu is covert activities, or if literally translated from the Japanese, "the art of stealing in." Ninjutsu came about from Japanese mystics during the rise of the samurai. It didn't exclude combat, but fighting was only a small part of a Ninja's total repertoire. Like so many fun things, the practice was eventually outlawed in the 17th century, but it was still practiced secretly for many years. Today it's only practiced as a form of martial art, as far as we know.

Who was Yoritomo?

Yoritomo was the leader of Japan during the medieval ages. In the late 1100s, he was the leader of the Minamoto clan. He set up Japan's very first warrior government, or shogunate, and was much lauded for uniting the country. As a result of this unification, Japan saw the birth of a long era of peace and stability.

How can someone become a samurai soldier?

These days, only special time travel will do the trick. The samurai began as a class of warriors in feudal Japan and stayed in power through the 17th century. But even if you could transport back to the days of the samurai, chances are you wouldn't have measured up. Few did. The honor of being a samurai was inherited, so unless you were a member of a certain elite class, you stood no chance of ever becoming a part of the ranks.

Within this hierarchy, you were expected to defend the land belonging to the aristocracy. You were given a special helmet and some armor, two swords, and a long list of what was expected of you. If you failed to live up to this list and were dishonored in any way, you were then expected to kill yourself. Being a samurai wasn't a lot of fun, but at least it was prestigious . . . and chicks dug them.

What was the Samurai Code?

Much like a western European chivalrous code of ethics, the Japanese samurai had a code of their own, which was orally transmitted from generation to generation. It was a code that evolved from a combination of strict military code, Zen Buddhism, Shintoism, and Confucianism. It was written down in the 17th century as *Way of the Warrior* (which is the translation of the Japanese word *Bushido)* by Yamaga Soko, a master of military and religion. The principles defined a way of living for the ruling class samurai and included instruction on being loyal, courageous, compassionate, honorable, respectful of life, and a sharp warrior. Most of the principles were about maintaining right-mindedness and upholding civic duty; however, some ideals had a darker side. Take ritualistic suicide—loyalty and honor sometimes drove samurai to this end. You can see remnants of the Samurai Code even in modern Japanese history, long after the last samurai lived. For instance, the overloyal acts of World War II kamikaze pilots were using the same honor and loyalty logic as their samurai predecessors. Some parts of the code are ingrained in the Japanese collective thought even today. A popular slogan for Japanese corporate cogs is "Business is war!" On the flip side, however, the Japanese tea ceremony is also a by-product of the Samurai Code. It embodies the principles of respect and honor of life.

TAKE A DIVE

What does "kamikaze" mean?

Kamikaze means "divine wind" in Japanese. The term was coined in 1281, referring to typhoons that wiped out a Mongol invasion fleet before it could arrive on Japan's shores. In the same way, the kamikaze hoped that their suicide missions would stop the Allies as they approached Japan.

I saw a photo of a kamikaze pilot, and he was wearing a helmet. Why, if you're expecting to die anyway, would you bother wearing a helmet?

You're working under the modern assumption that helmets are there to save you from death and injury. But helmets wouldn't do much in a plane crash, anyway. They were there for warmth, to hold the two-way radio for communication, and to protect your head from minor bangs that can occur from a sudden motion of the aircraft. You know, like the moment when you decide to go into a suicide dive toward an aircraft carrier.

Were kamikaze pilots suicidal, fanatical, brainwashed, or what?

Strange, but true: They have been described as being somewhat psychologically typical of Japanese youths at the time. A recurring theme in Japanese literature is that suicide of young people is a touchingly beautiful thing, like cherry blossoms falling before wilting, etc. Another theme was that it was honorable for soldiers to die for the country and emperor (who, at the time, was considered a god), and those who did so would dwell forever in a state of perpetual happiness. Some other interesting facts we discovered:

◆ The Japanese were losing the war and generally assumed that in defeat they would be treated as badly as they themselves had treated the Chinese and Koreans. Death was preferable to being conquered. (Imagine the embarrassment they must have experienced when they were eventually treated well in the occupation.)

◆ Because the Japanese lagged behind in war materials and trained soldiers, suicide missions started to make sense. Besides destroying warcraft, the Japanese high command believed that suicide attacks would so demoralize American soldiers and sailors that they'd find it hard to continue waging war.

- Another reason why the kamikaze program was instituted was because Japanese air strategy was becoming less and less effective. By the end of the war, most of Japan's experienced pilots were already dead. Training for Japanese airmen became so abbreviated that many could just barely fly a plane, let alone effectively wage war at the same time.

- A typical kamikaze attack involved 13 suicide planes and another thirteen planes as escorts.

- All kamikazes volunteered for the position. In fact, so many young men signed up that the authorities began accepting only those who scored highest in their school grades.

- Virtually all kamikazes were younger sons. Oldest sons were expected to take over the family business, so volunteering for a suicide mission would have been dishonorable.

- Japanese kamikaze pilots sank about 40 U.S. ships by purposely dive-bombing bomb-laden airplanes into them. The fact that Japan was willing to sacrifice both an airplane and a trained pilot was a sign of how desperately they wanted to stop the American onslaught.

How many kamikaze pilots were there?

There were about 4,000 kamikazes. Not all piloted planes—some were the drivers inside "smart bombs," torpedoes, and small, explosive-filled boats. Others volunteered to wear bombs on their bodies and throw themselves under the wheels of tanks.

Did any kamikazes survive their missions?

Despite their best intentions, some kamikazes did survive.

"HIROO, HIROO, IN COME FREE!"

When did the last Japanese soldier surrender in World War II?

In 1974. Somebody neglected to tell Lieutenant Hiroo Onoda that the war had ended. He stayed at his post on Lubang Island in the Philippines, and held out for 30 more years. When he finally was coaxed out by his long-retired commanding officer and learned the war was over, Onada was too overwhelmed to adapt to all of the changes. He retired to a quiet, rural ranch in Brazil.

What's the Warrior's Creed?

Following is dubbed the Warrior's Creed, found on just about every martial arts page on the Internet. The poem is heavy on religious principle, very Zen in nature, and attributed to an anonymous samurai from the 14th century. It might even be legitimate.

> I have no parents: I make the heavens and Earth my parents.
> I have no home: I make awareness my home.
> I have no life or death: I make the tides of breathing my life and death.
> I have no divine power: I make honesty my divine power.
> I have no means: I make understanding my means.
> I have no magic secrets: I make character my magic secret.
> I have no body: I make endurance my body.
> I have no eyes: I make the flash of lightning my eyes.
> I have no ears: I make sensibility my ears.
> I have no limbs: I make promptness my limbs.
> I have no strategy: I make "unshadowed by thought" my strategy.
> I have no design: I make "seizing opportunity by the forelock" my design.
> I have no miracles: I make right action my miracles.
> I have no principles: I make adaptability to all circumstances my principles.
> I have no tactics: I make emptiness and fullness my tactics.
> I have no talents: I make ready wit my talent.
> I have no friends: I make my mind my friend.

I have no enemy: I make carelessness my enemy.

I have no armor: I make benevolence and righteousness my armor.

I have no castle: I make immovable mind my castle.

I have no sword: I make absence of mind my sword.

QUIT YOUR BELLY ACHIN'

Say I'm a samurai and did something to bring dishonor to my master. Do I have to commit hara-kiri?

In the movies, most definitely. Realistically, it's not clear how often the practice of ritual suicide—or *seppuku*—was voluntarily carried out to clear a samurai's honor. The practice was more frequently used as a form of punishment, not as a completely voluntary act. What was involved is also often portrayed inaccurately: After donning white clothes and ritually washing himself, the warrior wrapped his sword in paper, then cut his own abdomen, an act generally called *hara-kiri* (loosely translated to mean "belly" and "cut"; maybe from the Japanese verb *kiru:* "to cut"). Following this, to end his excruciatingly painful suffering, the warrior's most trusted friend would chop his head off from behind. *Seppuku* would then be complete, and not a minute too soon.

BUILDING A SOLDIER FROM THE GROUND UP

Are the Chinese clay soldiers samurai?

No, samurai were strictly Japanese. The 1,000 terra-cotta soldiers, chariots, and horses were made, then buried with the first great emperor, Shi Huangdi, of the Qin Dynasty, a little over 2,000 years ago. Up until this time, it was commonplace for live soldiers, concubines, and others to be buried alive in the tombs of deceased emperors. Emperor Shi Huangdi is credited with ending the practice of live burial and replacing it with replicas symbolically guarding royal tombs.

The terra-cotta soldiers and horses, along with hundreds of other works of pottery and art, were accidentally uncovered in 1974 by a local farmer digging a well. Today he is sometimes found in the gift shop of the museum that's located in the foothills of the Lishan mountain, about 20 miles east of Xi'an. He'll give you an autograph and let you take his picture for a price.

THE GOOD, THE BAD, & THE MEDIEVAL

Western Europe during the Middle Ages is one of the most intriguing times in the history of civilization. The stories paint a picture of a land and time far away from our lives today: Lords and ladies, men in tights, witchcraft, religious fanaticism, life that was hard for most and cushy for the elite few. Hmm, maybe not so different from today after all.

MEDIEVAL SPREAD

What does "medieval" mean?

The word comes from two Latin words: *medium* and *aevum*. Respectively they mean "middle" and "age."

BECAUSE THEY HAD SO MANY KNIGHTS

Why do they call it the Dark Ages?

Historians don't call it that anymore; that term's as outdated as the Edsel. The disparaging label came about sometime during the Renaissance years (from the 1300s to the 1600s) when the common man could read and write, and science and technology were flourishing. Much of the scientific and technological legacies left by the ancient Romans had been lost in western Europe during the Middle Ages as political instability created a large educational and financial gap between the wealthiest lord and the poorest peasant. When Renaissance scholars compared the early Middle Ages—a time period from about 400 A.D. to 900 A.D.—with their own lives, the early time period seemed quite dark indeed.

Fortunately, this happened only in one small part of the world, western Europe. Various cultures—the Arab and Byzantine civilizations, for example—grew and advanced during this same time period and spread their knowledge all across the globe, eventually dragging even western Europe into the Renaissance as well.

What's the difference between Middle Ages, Dark Ages, and medieval?

Not much, although the Dark Ages traditionally refers to the first several centuries of the medieval period. Commonly, this whole medieval period extended from the end of the ancient Roman empire (somewhere around 400 A.D.) until the beginning of what is seen as "modern times" (about 1500 A.D.).

TAKING GREAT PAINS

Where did the rock group Iron Maiden get its name?

From the medieval torture device of the same name. The most famous of these devices was the iron maiden of Nuremberg. It was destroyed during WWII air attacks, but pictures remain. In essence, it was a standing box. Spikes protruded from the back of the box, and spikes were also fixed in the doors. It's suggested that the door was shut very slowly so as not to kill outright but to first inflict a great deal of pain before death was brought on. The iron maiden drew a lot of interest from 19th-century fiction writers. As a result, separating what is fact from what was imagined has proven difficult. We do know that it wasn't used as often as other means of torture or execution. As a matter of fact, the earliest record of use comes in the very late Middle Ages, in August 1515.

Was a Spanish Tickler the same as a French Tickler?

If only it were so, heretics of the late Middle Ages would've been very happy indeed. Alas, the Spanish Tickler, also known as a Cat's Paw, was a torture device. It was, in essence, a metal claw about the size of a large man's hand. It was used to literally rake a condemned person to a slow and painful death.

Ask! Where can I see pictures of torture devices from the Middle Ages?

SQUIRING MINDS WANT TO KNOW

Who invented the screwdriver?

No one knows exactly, but surely it was some poor squire, sick and tired of trying to figure out a way to tighten a knight into his armor with just his fingertips, or while searching through the grass for that dropped and missing bolt. But we do know the screwdriver was invented to bolt plates of armor around a knight.

What's the story behind the invention of the merry-go-round?

It's the oldest amusement ride around and was originally created during the Middle Ages as a device for training knights to joust. It took tragedy to popularize: When Catherine de Médicis' husband was killed during a jousting tournament in 1559, the merry-go-round began to take the place of actual knight-against-knight jousting as a safer alternative. Knights on the backs of wooden horses could spear rings or effigies of Turkish soldiers as they circled around and around. Jousting as a combat sport soon fell away entirely and the carousel's popularity grew when spectators also wanted a turn on the painted ponies. As homage to this early ride, some merry-go-round operators in Paris will still hang rings and offer riders a stick as they mount their rides to "joust" with, carrying on a centuries-old tradition.

HOT DOG! IT'S ARMOR

Armor looks really bulky. How did knights walk, much less mount their horses?

Walking wasn't an easy task, particularly once armor went from chain mail to plate mail, at which point knights (and their horses) were covered in huge chunks of metal all over their bodies. A knight's plate mail armor weighed upwards of 50 pounds for the full suit and got as heavy as 100 pounds, depending on the model. You can imagine that if he toppled over or slipped on a serf, he'd loll around on his back like an upturned beetle. This is no exaggeration.

Each battling knight had a squire to help him maintain uprightwardness. His squire assisted him in donning his armor and mounting his horse. When a knight was knocked off his steed, his squire would be at his side to help him get back on his feet again (quite literally). Knights also had a difficult time seeing; the helmet was so awkward, a page might have to inform his knight what was in front of him, or at the very least aim him in the right direction before the onset of battle.

So you can see how full plate armor quickly became an impractical uniform for war. For tournament jousting? Sure, because the battlers simply had to charge in one direction and see clearly enough to point. At the same time, their squires could rush out and attend to them once they were knocked on their breastplates or cruppers. However, if a squire were to help scoop his fallen knight out of the mud in battle he surely would be vulnerable—probably killed on the spot by the enemy. Most squires found it safer to simply run for the hills than stick around to rescue their fallen knights, and so plate mail fell out of favor. Besides, it became more and more difficult to produce usable armor that was also thick enough to keep those newfangled gun bullets from penetrating.

Why didn't knights just keep using chain mail?

Surprisingly, chain mail was really good at protecting against arrows and bludgeoning weapons. Soldiers who could afford and wear chain mail also wore leather tunics underneath, to keep the rings from being driven into their skin if they were clubbed. They relied heavily on their shields for defense as well. So chain mail was great—flexible, relatively light, and effective against most weapons.

So why did they abandon chain mail for plate armor? Simple. Have you ever seen what a crossbow can do? It's not pretty. It could shoot through the thin metal pieces of chain mail and straight through the leather. So plate mail was invented to protect against the crossbow, primarily. But as plate mail became thicker and thicker in order to withstand more and more powerful weapons, it became too bulky to be very effective in actually waging war, like wearing a tank.

Wasn't metal expensive back then? How could they afford the armor and weapons?

A full suit of plate armor—that is, plates of steel covering almost the entire body of the rider and his horse—could cost as much as a small farm at the time. The horse itself would cost the same amount, in today's money, as a luxury car. Much like playing polo and collecting Swiss bank accounts now, being a knight back then was reserved for only the wealthiest of sons.

Ask!

Where can I see pictures of medieval weapons?

NOW CROSS YOUR LEGS AND SIT UP STRAIGHT

Wasn't there a special way a knight who had served in a Crusade was prepared for burial?

Sort of. Traditionally, his legs were crossed instead of left straight.

VASSAL WHILE YOU WORK

What was a vassal?

A vassal was a knight who came from the bottom of the nobility and was bound in military service to his king. In exchange, his lord swore protection to him and gave him land to farm either for himself or commercially. Above him in social ranking were dukes, barons, earls, and counts.

The training of a vassal or knight began very early, at about the age of 7. He would go off to a knight school, of sorts, usually to the manor of a local knight who was sometimes his own father or uncle, where he would begin his apprenticeship by learning to handle small weaponry. Until he was about 15 or 16, he would learn etiquette, as well as how to hunt, ride, and use weapons. He would then advance to the position of squire, where he became a knight's aid. Over the next several years he'd take his lessons directly from his knight, learning the finer points of the job, including how to battle. At the end of this apprenticeship, the knight would then "knight" the squire. This new knight was then responsible for obtaining his own horse, armor, and weapons. He was then ready to serve his king.

WORDS CAN NEVER HURT ME

Where does the term "villain" come from?

Its root is found in the Old French word *vilain,* which in turn came from the Late Latin word *villanus.* Both mean "farm servant."

What's a scullery maid?

From Old French: *escueillier,* a place where bowls are kept. A scullery maid was (and still is, although the term isn't as common as it was in the Middle Ages) a kitchen helper.

A COMPLETE WASTE OF TIME

What toilets were used in medieval Europe?

An early Middle Ages anecdote notes that etiquette suggested a nobleman go "an arrow's flight" distance into the gardens before relieving himself. Unfortunately, records indicate that not all royalty felt the need to abide by such social rules. One shocked English nobleman's story tells of a visiting king who appallingly defecated wherever he wished throughout the castle. This same noble recounts a chat with a young noblewoman who was visiting his home. He was surprised to hear in midconversation a tinkling noise and then see an ever-growing puddle form beneath her dress.

But still, there were facilities of sorts, and the specifics of these were different, depending on where and when one lived in medieval Europe. For instance, castle homes were fortunate enough to have large concrete blocks tucked away in special and private locations. These blocks had a hole and chute called *garde robes* that led to the mote below. Peasants had to use either a bowl inside, which would then be emptied, or go directly outside to empty their bowels into a community cesspit, or hole. In the larger cities in the late Middle Ages, it became common to simply toss your excrement out the window into the street with a call of *"Garde l'eau!"* or "Gardy Loo!" as a warning to passersby below. During times of greater civic organization, city cleanup crews collected this waste, along with food waste, from the streets and sold it to farmers as fertilizer. However, the practice of tossing waste out on the streets was finally outlawed in 1372, when most realized it wasn't just an annoyance to be on a walk and suddenly be splattered with urine and excrement. It was a health hazard as well. Between the people and the horses, the smell of the larger European cities like London was unimaginable.

Ask!

What are the parts of a castle?

THOSE CLOTHES MAKE YOU LOOK MIDDLE AGED!

Did guys really wear tights in medieval times? Where'd they get tights, anyway? I thought tights were made out of nylon!

You watch too much TV. Tights on men of the Middle Ages were an invention of stage and screen, perhaps to give the actors something of the look of the age without going to the trouble of finding accurate costumes. Men, both the Anglo-Saxon pagans and the Christians of the early Middle Ages, sometimes wore leggings. These were made of linen or leather. They were either fitted (made to form to the leg) or they were bound by leather laces around the legs. Anglo-Saxons sometimes wrapped squares of leather around their legs with bindings, which gave a similar look.

Loose trousers—short and long—were also worn by men. The Anglo-Saxons called them *brec*, which is where our term "breeches" comes from.

Why did ladies wear those stupid-looking hats back in the Dark Ages?

If "stupid" means "pointy" or "heart-shaped," then the answer's fairly simple: style. The tall, pointed headdress was called a steeple cap and consisted of a wire frame, which was covered by linen or silk handkerchiefs. It was worn by the noble class only. Other headdress designs for the female nobility included the butterfly-shaped, the heart-shaped, and the traditional turban style.

Noble women and nuns also wore *wimples,* cloth caps that covered the head and forehead and tied under the neck. Many included what's called a *gorget:* an added piece of cloth that wraps around the neck.

GATHER 'ROUND

Who were the 12 knights of King Arthur's Round Table?

Depending on whose story you read, there may have been 12 or 24 or 150 or thousands. There are many tales of King Arthur's Round Table from different years, in both French and English. And of the traditional 12 knights, there are different lists of names. It's anyone's guess about the original group.

First, a little history. The Round Table is first mentioned in the work of the cleric named Wace, a renowned Norman poet from around 1155 A.D. In the piece titled *Le Roman de Brut,* he explained that the shape of the table kept Arthur's knights from fighting over who had the seat of honor. The Round Table made it so that everyone and no one had the best seat or was considered more worthy than the rest.

Over the years, the Round Table developed into an almost mythical object. In the English translation of Wace's work, the table was so large it could seat up to 1,600 men and held magical powers beyond simply resolving conflict among the knights. As large as it was, it could still be folded up and carried on horseback. (If you could happen to find one of these on the Internet, let us know because we'd like one, too.)

The more popular version of the story has the table holding enough spaces for 12 of the bravest, most honorable knights. The magic number 12 is, of course, borrowed from the image of Christ's apostles. Taking this imagery even further, in one version of the tale, an empty seat always remains open, representing Judas' absence, as is portrayed in the Last Supper, or Jesus (or the coming Messiah) on Passover, depending on whom you ask. This empty seat was called the Siege Perilous and was reserved for the knight who would be so holy that he'd find the Holy Grail. Later, Sir Galahad's name appears in the empty place as being worthy of sitting there.

While you may well get a different set of 12, depending on what source you consult, here are the more common of those Arthurian knights who were seated in the round: Gawain, Ban, Bedivere, Ector, Gareth, Kay, Lancelot, Launfal, Palomides, Sagramore, Ywain, Galahad, Bors, and Perceval. The latter three are the ones who, according to legend, eventually uncovered the Holy Grail.

Ask!

Where can I find a copy of Monty Python's The Search for the Holy Grail?

OUR FAVORITE DISASTERS

These are the things that B-grade movies are made of. They instill fear and dread, the thought of being swallowed by the earth, drowned by the sea, or buried under molten lava and molasses. Molasses? Read on to learn the facts behind some of history's most well known (and not so well known) disasters.

THAT SINKING FEELING

What was the song that the* Titanic *band played as the ship went down?

"*Songe d'Automne,*" also called "Dream of Autumn," by Archibald Joyce (1908) could've been the last song the band played on the

Titanic. Or it could've been the hymn "Nearer My God to Thee," the bandleader's favorite and the tune many survivors remember hearing last. The truth is that no one will ever know for certain (including the directors of the blockbuster hit movie *Titanic* who went with the hymn) because the band members continued to play even as the ship went down. They did this apparently to reduce panic, and by all accounts their bravery helped save lives.

One survivor—a member of the crew, Harold Bride—remembered the incident distinctly: "The way the band kept playing was a noble thing. I heard it first while still we were working wireless, when there

> **What was Archibald Joyce's nickname?**
> The English Waltz King.

was a ragtime tune for us, and the last I saw of the band, when I was floating out in the sea with my lifebelt on, it was still on deck playing "Autumn." How they ever did it I cannot imagine."

How many passengers were on the Titanic? How many survived?

There were 2,227 passengers aboard the ship. Of those, only 375 survived.

How many ships since the Titanic have struck icebergs and gone down?

At this writing, none.

If not an iceberg, what did the Exxon Valdez oil ship hit in Alaska?

A reef. They have them in Alaska, too, you know.

CHICAGO CATTLE-CLYSM

Did a cow really cause the Chicago fire?

No, probably not, although the fire did start in the O'Leary's barn. There's no reason to believe the fire was anything more than the result of an extraordinary dry spell of weather mixed with the practice of keeping dry wood chips around as a cheap source of fuel. A cigarette, a match, an ember from a burning stove nearby, or even spontaneous combustion would have been more than enough to set the blaze going. Incidentally, a much bigger, more deadly fire happened on the exact same night in Peshtigo,

Wisconsin; it was started by railroad workers clearing a way for new tracks. As a result of the dry air, a small brush fire turned into a blazing inferno. Before the fire went out almost a week later it had burned over 1.2 million acres and caused more than $169 million dollars worth of damage—about the same dollar amount of the property lost in the Chicago blaze. On top of that, over 1,200 people were killed by the Wisconsin fire—four times as many as the Chicago fire. It didn't get as much publicity, though.

Why did the Chicago fire of 1871 do so much damage?

Besides the dryness in the air and the wood chips, the houses were old, wooden, and packed in tightly. There may have been little anyone could have done to prevent the disaster. However, it didn't help that the firemen were misdirected when the initial call came in. Furthermore, they had been busy with another huge fire the day before and were exhausted. By the time they reached the site, the blaze was way beyond control.

CLAIM TO FLAME

Which was worse: the Great London Fire or the Chicago fire?

The 1666 London fire burned four-fifths of the city and an additional 63 acres outside the city walls. The London fire burned longer, covered more land, and wreaked more architectural devastation: London's Guildhall, the Custom House, the Royal Exchange, and beautiful St. Paul's Cathedral. Still, the Chicago fire was worse in some ways, including lives lost. It's reported that only 16 people died in the London fire because it burned slowly and gave enough warning for most people to escape. The fast-moving Chicago fire claimed between 250 and 300 lives and leveled several Chicago neighborhoods—a total of 2,150 acres in less than two days. Both great fires caused mass devastation with few rewards, save an architectural revitalization following the blaze and a good story about a cow.

One irrefutable bright spot came on the heels of the Great London Fire: After hundreds of years of periodic devastation, the Black Plague was finally wiped out. It had resurfaced again two years prior to the blaze, in 1664. However, after the fire, incidences suddenly declined and fizzled out, never to resurface again. It's believed that because the fire burnt everything to the ground, it took with it the old, damp breeding grounds of the plague rats, saving literally thousands of human lives in the long run.

GEORGIE, PORGIE, PUDDING & PIE

How did the Great London Fire start?

It's reported that the 1666 fire that swept London was actually started by King Charles II's baker, Thomas Farrinor, who accidentally went to bed with his oven still burning.

The phrase "from pudding to pie" comes directly from the Great Fire of London. Farrinor's house was situated on Pudding Lane. Pie Lane is located on the other side of the city where the fire finally stopped. So those clever and punny Brits used "from pudding to pie" to mean the whole bloomin' city from then on.

THE TIDE IS HIGH, BUT I'M HOLDIN' ON

What is it that the Chinese call "China's Sorrow"?

The Huang He or Yellow River. Flooding has been a problem for years, but with deforestation of the mountains in the north, the flood lines have widened and changed the course of the river several times.

The worst, most sorrowful flood on record happened in 1931. The waters began to rise in July, and by November of that year, more than 40,000 square miles had been flooded, leaving 80 million people homeless, and from disease, famine, and drowning, close to one million dead.

SHOW ME YOUR BUBOES, BABY, AND I'LL CHECK YOU FOR THE PLAGUE

Why was the Black Death also called the Bubonic Plague?

Initially it was dubbed Black Death because of the black sores that developed on the bodies of the afflicted. However, once a connection was made with the swollen lymph nodes called "buboes," "Bubonic Plague" seemed a fitting and accurate label for the disease.

What was the worst plague in human history?

The Black Death that ran through China and across Europe in the 14th century is considered the worst plague in recorded history. Depending on the way the virus was contracted, 70 to 90 percent of those exposed to the plague died from it. During a five-year period, from 1347 to 1352, over 25 million people in Europe alone were wiped out.

That was the worst *plague*; however, it wasn't the worst *epidemic*. What's the difference? The plague is a specific *bacterial* infection, but many of the worst epidemics have been caused by *viruses*. The worst epidemic was not a plague but a flu that swept the world from 1918 to 1919. The first reported case was in Kansas in 1918, and from there it spread like wildfire. Eighteen months later, the virus vanished as mysteriously as it had appeared, after between 25 and 37 million people had died from the disease. At no other time in recorded history have so many people died from one affliction in so little time.

How long did it take someone to die who caught the Bubonic Plague?

From the time of exposure (flea bite, animal bite, or exposure to mucus) to the onset of the first symptoms (headache, fever, nausea, aching, and swollen buboes) took about six days on average. The next stage—hemorrhaging and respiratory problems stemming from severe pneumonia—came quickly, usually causing death within a day or two. Nowadays, luckily, bacterial infections can usually be wiped out by antibiotics.

ASH FROM A HOLE IN THE GROUND

How many people did Vesuvius kill?

Which time? Mount Vesuvius, the active volcano on the coast of Italy, has erupted more than 50 times since burying the cities of Pompeii and Herculaneum in 79 A.D. It's estimated that the first reported eruption killed about 3,400 people, mostly by burying them in thick pumice deposits. From that date, and probably before that date, Mount Vesuvius erupted every 100 years until about

1037 A.D., when it went quiet. Almost 600 years later, however (in 1631), it surprised nearby inhabitants again by erupting and causing over 4,000 deaths in the area. It was during the cleanup from this eruption that the ruins of ancient Pompeii were first uncovered.

Is Vesuvius the worst volcano in history?

No. The deadliest volcano in history award goes to Mount Tambora, Indonesia, for its eruption in 1815. Journalist Judith Coan for Discovery.com describes it like this:

> The largest eruption during the last two centuries, as well as the deadliest volcano in recorded history, Mount Tambora exploded April 10–11, 1815. It killed an estimated 92,000 people. Almost 80,000 of the victims died of starvation brought on by the agricultural devastation in the volcano's wake. The eruption and the resulting massive clouds of dust and ash affected most of the Northern Hemisphere, causing unusually cool temperatures and failed crops in 1816—sometimes referred to as "the year without a summer."

Has Mount St. Helens in Washington ever had a larger eruption than the one in 1980?

According to those who study these things, there was one around 2000 B.C. that was larger. Mount St. Helens has been an active volcano for over 40,000 years, and scientists have predicted that another eruption could happen in the next 20 or 30 years.

Were there any survivors of the 1902 volcanic eruption of Mount Pelee, on the island of Martinque?

Yes, there were two. The other 29,000 inhabitants were wiped out.

Ask! Where can I see volcanoes live on the web?

GOOD STORIES WITH A TWIST

Why is the tornado scale that measures the severity of a tornado called the F scale? Is it related to musical tones? Does it stand for "funnel"? I give up.

Good. It's actually named after the meteorologist who came up with the scale. His name was Tetsuya Theodore (Ted) Fujita, or

"Mr. Tornado" to those who knew him. The "F" came from his last name.

How fast is an F-4 tornado?
About 207 to 260 mph.

ANOTHER BIG GAS BAG GOES DOWN IN FLAMES

What's listed on the official report as the cause of the fire that destroyed the Hindenburg in 1937?

St. Elmo's Fire, or, to a layperson: static electricity. In actuality, it was probably the highly combustible hydrogen used to fuel the air ship. Why would the Nazis stupidly use hydrogen if it's so flammable, you may be asking? Because times were tough and the U.S. had cornered the market on helium, charging exorbitant prices for it. Most forewent safety to save a little dough; the Nazis were no exception.

WIPE OUT!

What was the name of the dam at Johnstown, Pennsylvania, that broke loose and flooded the town?

It shares a name with J. R. Ewing's homestead: South Fork.

Has a tidal wave ever hit the U.S.?

Tidal waves, more accurately called tsunamis, have hit the U.S. several times, most often in Hawaii or Alaska. However, California has been hit a couple of times in the last hundred years as well. The most deadly, but surprisingly obscure, tsunami to strike the contiguous U.S. took place in 1964. A record-shattering earthquake in Alaska was the catalyst for a series of huge waves— at least one (in Shoup Bay, Valdez Inlet) officially measured 67 meters high—that crashed into the western U.S. coast. All in all, 120 people lost their lives throughout Canada, Alaska, Oregon, Washington, and California. The deaths included 106 Alaskan residents and four campers on a beach in Newport, Oregon. Crescent City, California, was engulfed in a wave and 11 people were killed. Another man in Klamath, California, drowned.

In 1946, Hawaii was caught relatively unaware by a

devastating tsunami. One hundred and seventy-three people were killed, prompting the foundation of the Pacific Tsunami Warning System (PTWS), a system that watches for tsunamis and attempts to give timely warnings of their approach to all U.S. regions in the Pacific.

> **What does tsunami literally mean in Japanese?**
> *Tsu* (harbor) *nami* (wave).

SHAKE, RATTLE, AND ROLL

Which San Francisco earthquake was more costly: the one in 1906 or 1989?

In dollars and cents, the 1989 Loma Prieta quake was the costliest at $5.9 billion, whereas the 1906 San Francisco quake totaled a mere $400 million. Some would argue that in today's money, that would equal about $7.6 billion dollars. However, in today's money, the 1989 damage would equal about $8.2 billion.

How many people were killed in the 1906 San Francisco earthquake?

From the quake directly and from the burning aftermath, about 3,000 people. At the time, the San Francisco city government downplayed the numbers and blamed them primarily on the fire, figuring that tourists and newcomers would be less frightened by fire as a familiar danger than by terrifyingly unfamiliar earthquakes.

Was the 1906 San Francisco earthquake the deadliest U.S. natural disaster?

No, Hurricane Frederick, which pounded Galveston, Texas, in 1900, holds that honor. It left over 6,000 dead.

What's the worst earthquake in recorded history?

It happened on January 23, 1556, in Shansi, China. The quake killed over 830,000 people. Compare that to some of the other "big ones" throughout history:

- ◆ Tangshan, China, 1976—officially 255,000 dead; unofficial estimates put it at around 600,000

- ◆ Aleppo, Syria, 1138—230,000 dead

- Xining, China, 1927—200,000 dead
- Messina, Italy, 1908—70,000–100,000 dead
- Peru, 1970—66,000 dead

The Mississippi quake of 1811 ranks up there as well: The power of the quake was so forceful that it changed the course of the Mississippi River. However, there's no record of any human life lost. Maybe next time.

A STICKY SWEET ENDING

What was the Boston Molasses Flood?

That's exactly what it was: a molasses flood. Just after noon on January 15, 1919, at the United States Alcohol Company in Boston, a fifty-eight-foot tall, 90-feet wide steel structure, holding 2.5 million gallons of hot molasses, burst open. Metal flew everywhere, and a geyser of sticky, boiling liquid spewed up and out. It quickly filled a loading pit in the factory, smothering those standing nearby. The molasses pushed freight cars off the tracks and pulled the front of a neighboring house completely off, killing its inhabitants. Lunching workers at the nearby public works department, casually sitting around a table, were boiled and smothered to death when molasses poured into their building. The entire fire station was washed down toward the ocean.

When all was said and done, 21 people had come to a sticky demise. The lawsuits that followed cost the molasses factory about a million dollars in damages. It was ruled, after a lengthy investigation, that the tank hadn't been strong enough to hold that much molasses. In addition, rising temperatures in Boston had increased the danger.

"History is mostly about killin' people," observed television's Theodore "Beaver" Cleaver. And the Beav was right, of course. There's nothing like war and mass destruction to leave a big enough impression on observers that they'd bother writing about it . . . and that's history.

THE BRITISH INVASION

My history teacher says that the United States has never been invaded by a foreign power. Why not?

Well, we *could* tell you that it's because of our (mostly) friendly neighbors and the difficulties of crossing an ocean with an invasion force large enough to do the job. We *could* do that, but instead we'd rather cast scorn because your teacher is so very wrong.

And we're not just talking about minor invasions here, either, like the Japanese bombings along the West Coast, the German sabotage squad's landing in New Jersey, or Pancho Villa's attack on New Mexico. No, this was a full-fledged incursion where an enemy force burned the Capitol and sacked the White House, nearly capturing the president and first lady in the process. It happened, of course, during the War of 1812, when England stormed borders and nearly got the chance to reclaim the colony it had given up less than four decades earlier.

WARS OF PIGS & PIGSKINS

Is it true that there once was a war about a soccer game?

Well, sort of. It's true that during a particularly rough championship *futbol* match between El Salvador and Honduras in 1969, people rioted in the streets and the stadium. When the Salvadorans won the championship on a disputed call, Honduras declared war. Before a cease-fire was negotiated by international authorities, 2,000 people were killed, much of El Salvador's industrial base had been bombed, and the Salvadoran army had marched 25 miles into Honduran territory.

However, it's too simple to say that the Soccer War was really about a soccer game. That's like concluding from the Boston Tea Party that the American Revolution was a dispute about hot beverages. As with many wars with unlikely triggering events, the *real* reason for the Soccer War was simmering grievances that had been ready to erupt for years. Throughout the 1960s, there had been conflict between the two countries about Salvadoran peasants encroaching along the Honduras border.

What was the weirdest cause of war?

There were many. Along with the Soccer War, here are some other wars you might want to consider while contemplating the tragic foolishness of humanity:

- **The War of the Oaken Bucket (1325–37).** This twelve-year war between the Italian cities of Modena and Bologna was triggered by the theft of a wooden bucket by the soldiers of Modena. Thousands of people from both sides were killed.

- **The War of the Whiskers (1152–1453).** When France's King Louis VII returned from the Crusades clean-shaven, his wife— the lovely but not completely loveable Eleanor of Aquitane— told him he was ugly without it. When he refused to grow it back, she divorced him and married King Henry II of England. Adding injury to insult, she demanded the transfer of her dowry to her new husband, which included two provinces in what is now southern France. Louis refused; Henry declared war; and the War of the Whiskers turned into a conflict that lasted 301 years.

- **The War of Jenkins' Ear (1739–43).** Captain Robert Jenkins appeared before the British Parliament in 1739, displaying the remains of his left ear and demanding war against Spain. He was a shipper who had been caught smuggling illicit cargo by the Spanish Coast Guard in South America. Jenkins seriously insulted the customs agent, and in response the man cut off his ear and handed it to him. Because of this affront to an Englishman, the British were outraged and kept the ear displayed in Parliament for years as a reminder of how the Spanish could not be trusted. A few years later, when war between England and Spain was officially declared, it became known as the War of Jenkins' Ear.

- **Toledo War (1835–36).** Thanks to faulty maps, both Michigan and Ohio claimed the city of Toledo. The issue came to a head in September 1835 when both states sent troops to defend their claims. After a cold-war standoff that lasted throughout the frigid midwestern winter, a shooting war was averted during the June thaw of 1836 by President Andrew Jackson. With his deal, both sides won: He ruled that Ohio would get Toledo, but as a consolation prize, Michigan would get what would become its Upper Peninsula (arguably a much better deal). The only loser wasn't even part of the war: Wisconsin, which had already claimed the territory that Jackson was so casually handing over to Michigan.

- ◆ **The War of the Stray Dog (1925).** On the tense border between Greece and Bulgarian Macedonia, a dog strayed away from the Greek soldier who had adopted it and crossed the border. The soldier chased after it and was shot by a Bulgarian guard. Infuriated, Greek soldiers stormed across the border. More than fifty soldiers were killed before the League of Nations intervened and stopped the hostilities.

And then, of course, there were the pig wars (see below).

What were the Pig Wars?

There were no fewer than three different conflicts known by that name in three different times and places. Although none of them actually resulted in shots being fired, each *could* have had serious ramifications, and there are some historians who say that Pig War #3 probably helped plant the seeds for the events that triggered World War I.

- ◆ **Pig War #1.** This pig war was a high-level diplomatic rupture between the French government and the Republic of Texas in 1841. It started as a private dispute between Richard Bullock, an Austin hotel owner who owned a herd of pigs, and Alphonse Dubois de Saligny, the French chargé d'affaires. Dubois de Saligny complained that Bullock's pigs were invading his yard and house and eating his crops, food, bed linens, and even his diplomatic papers. Bullock charged that the French official's servant had killed some of his pigs; he gave the servant a good thrashing and threatened to do the same to the diplomat. Between demands of official sanction and claims of diplomatic immunity, Dubois de Saligny broke off diplomatic relations, moved to Louisiana, and issued a series of stern threats claiming that terrible retributions would soon be raining down on Austin from the French government. However, the French government, while it supported its diplomat in the dispute, wasn't about to send troops to teach impertinent Texan yahoos a lesson.

Eventually, after a lot of Franco-Texan bluster, things got sorted out, and Dubois de Saligny returned to his post.

♦ **Pig War #2.** As a result of this pig war, there was almost yet another war between the United States and Britain. By 1859, all of the border disputes between the United States and Canada had long been resolved, except for one: San Juan Island, which straddled the border between Washington State and Vancouver Island. Both countries claimed it, and neither was willing to give an inch. Tensions already ran high between the Americans and Canada's British administrators on the island, but then one day in June a runaway pig brought the tensions to the squealing point.

An American settler named Lyman Cutler found a pig rooting up his garden and shot it. When he tried to find the owner, he discovered that it belonged to the powerful, Canadian-based British colonial Hudson's Bay Company. He offered to pay for the dead pig but balked when company officials claimed it was a special breed worth $100 (more than $2,000 in today's money). British authorities threatened to arrest him. In response, Cutler appealed to the American government for protection. And that was the beginning of a comedy that stopped just this side of tragedy.

The American army post in Oregon sent in a 66-man unit. It landed and moved to occupy a spot near the Hudson's Bay Company's wharf. The British colonial governor called in three British battleships to lurk menacingly off the coast. In response, the Americans called in more troops. The British did the same. Two months later, 461 American men and 14 cannons were prepared to take on the British force of five battleships bearing 167 guns and 2,140 troops.

Despite their superior numbers, the British authorities wisely held off arresting Cutler or disarming the American troops while waiting for orders. Meanwhile, word of the standoff finally got back to Washington, D.C. A near-apoplectic James Buchanan sent General Winfield Scott to defuse the situation, hoping it wasn't too late.

It wasn't. Scott quickly rebuked the local army commander and arranged a meeting with the British governor. Both sides agreed to de-escalate, withdrawing all but a token force of soldiers from each side. Ten years later, the matter went to arbitration with Kaiser Wilhelm I of Germany acting as mediator. He ruled for the Americans; San Juan Island became part of Washington, and the Pig War ended with only one casualty—the pig.

◆ **Pig War #3.** The third pig war took place between Serbia and the Austria–Hungary empire in 1906. It was an economic war in which Vienna tried to take advantage of the fact that it was the main trading partner of the Serbs. Belgrade, faced with the threat of an embargo, responded by making a deal to sell its pork to the Germans, leaving the Austrians with shortages of chops, ham, bacon, and sausages. This so enraged the Austrians that they threatened war. The Russians threatened to jump in on the Serbs' side; in response, the Germans threatened to support their Austrian allies—and World War I almost started eight years early. Eventually, though, things went back to a tense stalemate, and Serbia began trading with the Austrians again.

This was another pig war in which not a shot was fired. That didn't come until 1914 when an assassin in Sarejevo killed an Austrian–Hungarian archduke, setting off WWI.

THE ODDS OF WAR

This may sound morbid, but in which major American war did a soldier have the best chance of survival?

The easiest way to figure out the odds of surviving any particular war is to compare the number of people who served with the number of people who died. For the sake of encompassing all the dangers of war—bullets, bombs, epidemics, mistreatment in POW camps, deaths while traveling to and from, even getting run down by 19-year-old jeep drivers—we'll consider all deaths that occurred "in service." Here are our best estimates for the odds of survival for a soldier in the U.S. Army, according to statistics provided by the Department of Veterans Affairs:

Revolutionary War
Participants: 290,000
Deaths in service: 4,000
Chance of dying: 1 chance in 22.3

War of 1812
Participants: 287,000
Deaths in service: 2,000
Chance of dying: 1 in 143.5

Indian Wars
Participants: 106,000
Deaths in service: 1,000
Chance of dying: 1 in 106

Mexican War
Participants: 79,000
Deaths in service: 13,000
Chance of dying: 1 in 6.5 (only 1,800 died in battle; many more died from smallpox and syphilis)

Civil War
Participants: 2,213,000 (United States side only)
Deaths in service: 364,000
Chance of dying: 1 in 6

Spanish-American War
Participants: 392,000
Deaths in service: 11,000
Chance of dying: 1 in 35.6

World War I
Participants: 4,744,000
Deaths in service: 116,000
Chance of dying: 1 in 40.9

World War II
Participants: 16,535,000
Deaths in service: 406,000
Chance of dying: 1 in 40.7

Korean War
Participants: 6,807,000
Deaths in service: 55,000
Chance of dying: 1 in 123.8

Vietnam War
Participants: 9,200,000
Deaths in service: 109,000
Chance of dying: 1 in 84.4

Gulf War
Participants: 3,900,000
Deaths in service: 8,200
Chance of dying: 1 in 475.6

America's Total Wars
Participants: 41,902,000
Deaths in service: 1,089,200
Average chance of dying: 1 in 38.5

Put it all together, and you'll quickly note that the safest war for an American soldier was the Gulf War. The most dangerous was the Civil War: a soldier's chance for survival was only 1 in 6—the same odds as playing Russian roulette with a six-shooter.

WAITING FOR THE ROBERT E. LEE

What was the bloodiest battle fought on American soil?

The Battle of Gettysburg. In three days 5,662 soldiers were confirmed killed, 10,584 were missing, and 27,203 were wounded.

As mentioned, the Civil War was the bloodiest for Americans. More Americans died in that war than in all of its other wars combined. How bad was it? About 618,000 soldiers died on both sides of the conflict, plus a large number of civilians who were routinely terrorized and killed by both the North and South. Some historians put the total deaths as high as one million (about 8% of the entire American/Confederate population at the time). Direct and indirect costs of the war totaled over $15 billion dollars at the time—the equivalent of more than $164 billion in today's dollars—and left the South financially damaged for generations thereafter.

Gettysburg was a small village surrounded by Union troops. Why did the Confederates bother trying to take it?

A Confederate soldier found a local newspaper that announced a sale on a storehouse of shoes in Gettysburg. Major General Henry Heth decided that too many of his soldiers were marching barefoot, so he sent his 7,500 men down to take possession of the warehouse and the shoes therein. At a crossroads about three miles from the town, the barefoot battalion stubbed its toe on a brigade of Union soldiers, and the battle began.

IT'S GENERAL EWELL'S ARMY, MEN—LOAD WITH BIRDSHOT

Who was the Civil War general who thought he was a bird?

Ah, that would be Confederate General Richard Ewell, known as "Old Baldy" to his men. He was at Gettysburg under Robert E. Lee and served admirably. However, he was a true eccentric, partial to surreal jokes and nonsensical nonsequiturs. But there may have been a reason for his very odd sense of humor: General Ewell might have been delusional. Persistent stories say he believed himself to be a bird, eating grains of wheat and sunflower seeds for meals. There were persistent stories from soldiers on guard duty claiming that the General would spend many hours in his tent quietly chirping to himself.

The accounts could have been true or they may have been mere tall tales hatched from the fact that he resembled a bird in several significant ways: He had a beaklike nose; he hopped around camp like a parakeet on one leg (he'd lost the other in an earlier battle); he had a high voice, which would degenerate into an unrecognizable staccato when he got excited; he had a bald head, which he had a habit of tilting in a parrotlike way. Finally, he subsisted almost entirely

Ask! How much of Atlanta did General Sherman destroy?

on frumenty, a dish of hulled wheat boiled in milk and sugar.

Regardless of these quirks, he was by all accounts a good general who was beloved by his men.

GENERAL INFORMATION

How did Stonewall Jackson die?

The Confederate general was shot by his own men as he returned from a battle near Chancellorsville, VA. And it was his own darned fault. Before he left to scout out the battle lines, he had ordered the soldiers guarding the front lines to "shoot first, ask questions later" if anyone approached. A while later, he came crashing through the underbrush without identifying himself first. They followed orders, and Jackson suffered a mortal wound.

Still, it wasn't the most embarrassing death of a Civil War officer. That honor goes to Union General John Sedgwick at the Battle of Spotsylvania. When a distant Confederate sharpshooter started firing, Sedgwick's men scurried for cover. "What, what men!" he called out. "This will never do; dodging for single bullets! I tell you, they could not hit an elephant at this distance!" One of his aides later bore witness to what happened next: "Before the smile which accompanied these words had departed from his lips, and as he was in the act of resuming conversation with the staff officer by his side, there was a sharp whistle of a bullet, terminating in a dull, soft sound; and he fell slowly and heavily to the earth." Struck in the face, Sedgwick died instantly. A decade later, some of his surviving men put up a monument to him on the spot. Coincidentally, it was larger than an elephant.

Is it true that the slang term for a prostitute, "hooker," originated with soldiers serving under the Civil War general, Joseph Hooker?

No. The term was already in use in 1845, two decades before the Civil War. A more reasonable origin for the term comes from *Webster's New World Dictionary*, which says that a hooker was "originally a resident of Corlear's Hook, an area in New York City, whose brothels were frequented by sailors."

Where did the term "sideburns" come from?

Union General Ambrose Burnside's fuzzy and odd-looking whiskers inspired people to call that kind of facial hair "burnsides." As time passed, wits whimsically reversed the name into "sideburns," which sort of makes sense because they're on the side of the face. The name stuck.

CIRCULATION WARS

Who was it who said, "You furnish the pictures and I'll furnish the war"?

None other than William Randolph Hearst. His newspapers were notorious for finding news, even where there was none.

By 1897, things were tense between the United States and Spain, and rumors of war were widespread. Fueled by patriotism and a desire for inflammatory front-page material for his paper, Hearst sent illustrator Frederic Remington to Cuba in the hopes of getting exclusive views of the war's onset. When nothing happened, Remington asked to come home, and that's when Hearst issued that now-famous promise.

His statement wasn't too farfetched. The *Examiner* and other newspapers soon swayed public opinion that colonial Spain needed to leave Cuba and make way—as other Latin American countries had—for U.S. expansion. Not long after Hearst cabled these words, the American ship, the *Maine*, blew up from a faulty boiler. The American public was so inflamed that it wasn't hard to get them to believe that Spain had bombed the U.S. battleship. The Spanish-American War began, and Hearst got his front-page stories for weeks afterward.

TIME IN A BATTLE

How long did the Hundred Years' War last?

It was fought over 126 years (1337–1453). The British won most of the battles, but the French won the war.

How long was the Six-Day War?

Well, it wasn't exactly six days, but it was close. For Israel, it went on for 132 hours and 30 minutes—a little over five and a half days from start to finish. However, Egypt saw the war's end after four days, and Jordan after three.

THOSE CRAZY KIDS

What happened to the kids who went on the Children's Crusade?

The Crusades of medieval western Europe became progressively uglier as centuries passed; gold and lives were squandered, and yet the Crusaders were no closer to wresting the Holy Land from the infidel Muslims. In 1202, Crusaders ransacked Christian churches and Eastern European villages, much to the embarrassment of the Church and their communities back home. Morale in western Europe was at an all-time low.

It was in this atmosphere that two young boys emerged from the countryside of western Europe to act as God's warriors. Stephen was a young shepherd boy from Cloyes, France. Devout and eager, he claimed to have received a message from Jesus that he was to walk to Jerusalem and crush the infidels. Stephen soon managed to attract thousands of French boys to his cause, all hoping to change the world and right the wrongs of the Crusaders before them. Parents cried and begged them not to go, but church officials, by many accounts, fully encouraged these youths in their quest.

At the same time, a similar scene was being played out in Germany. Nicholas, a local peasant boy from Cologne, said he had received specific instructions from a cross of lights in the sky. He managed to gather at least 7,000 young people to his cause. Like lambs to slaughter, the two groups of unarmed children marched off to reclaim the Holy Sepulcher.

It's a toss-up for which group fared worse. Most of the German children either froze to death or slid off the mountains trying to get through the Alps. The French children suffered from disease and hunger during their long march. When they reached the Mediterranean Sea, they were disappointed to discover that the sea did not part and let them walk across, as Stephen had prophesied. Finally, seven ships were supplied by two rich merchants to carry the boys across the the Mediterranean. Two of them sank in storms with 1,400 children aboard. The other five reached land on the other side but nowhere near the Holy Land, alas. The sailors had changed course to Egypt where they sold the boys into slavery. Many of them were put to death when they refused to convert to Islam.

Meanwhile, the German children who survived passage over the Alps split into smaller groups, each looking for the passage to Palestine. Some arrived at the Italian port of Genoa with no means of transportation. Others just disappeared into the countryside to fates unknown. Of the thousands that set out from France and Germany, only a hundred or two were ever heard from again. Some historians theorize that the tale of the Pied Piper of Hamelin—who magically led an entire German village of children away, never to be seen again—was an allegorical history of the parents' and villagers' deep sense of loss over their children who went off to the Children's Crusade.

SOUNDS LIKE A TYPICAL COLLEGE APARTMENT

What was "the Black Hole of Calcutta"?

In the year 1756, British and Indian troops were busy warring when Indians managed to capture a British fort in Calcutta. The troops locked their captives into a 14 by 18 foot room for the night. A British survivor named John Holwell charged that 123 of 146 men suffocated in the room. While convenient for rallying anti-Indian sentiment among the English, the figures are probably historically inaccurate (although it might've *seemed* that crowded inside the room). Historians who checked British military records say that the figures tallied by the Indians are probably more accurate: 43 prisoners of war panicked in the dark, killing 15 of their countrymen.

Which war was Lord Alfred Tennyson writing about in "The Charge of the Light Brigade"?

The Crimean War, the same war that made Florence Nightingale famous.

WHAT MOM WOULDN'T BE HONORED?

What were the names of the planes that dropped the atomic bombs?

The B-29 that dropped "Little Boy" on Hiroshima on August 6, 1945, was commanded by Colonel Paul Tibbets, Jr. He had painted the aircraft the day before with his mother's name, *Enola Gay.* The B-29 that carried "Fat Man" to Nagasaki was known as *Bockscar* (often misspelled as Bock's Car) because it was normally flown by Captain Frederick C. Bock. On August 9, Bock flew an observatory plane called *The Great Artiste,* and Major Charles W. Sweeney used his plane to drop the bomb on Nagasaki.

NOT IN MY BACKYARD

Besides Hawaii, were any other American states attacked during World War II?

Well, technically, Hawaii wasn't a state yet. Neither was Alaska in 1942, so Japan's invasion and occupation of the Attu and Kiska in the Aleutian Islands doesn't quite count, either. (America fought back, and Japan retreated from the islands the following year.)

However, Japan *did* attack an oil well in southern California, a military depot in Oregon, and some tankers and a forest in Washington State. In early 1944, a German reconnaissance aircraft flew over New York City, photographing possible targets for long-range bombers. In response, American bombers were sent to destroy the plant where the bombers were being made.

MAN'S INHUMANITY

How many people died at Auschwitz?

Best estimates are that about four million people died there from overwork, starvation, and poison gas. Rudolf Hess, the death camp's commandant, called it "the largest human slaughterhouse that history has ever known" and estimated that as many as 9,000 people a day died in the gas chambers.

What did Hitler have in mind for England if Germany's invasion plans were successful?

Pretty much the same as every other country that the Nazis conquered: Kill the intelligentsia and enslave the rest. For example, when the Nazis took over Poland, they quickly liquidated more than half of Poland's college graduates. In *Orders Concerning the Organization and Function of Military Government in England,* a plan drawn up in 1940, the German government included a list of celebrated British writers and thinkers who were to be tracked down and killed immediately. The list included Bertrand Russell, H. G. Wells, J. B. Priestley, C. P. Snow, and Noel Coward. Meanwhile, large numbers of British men between the ages of 17 and 45 were to be shipped to Germany for slave labor.

Why didn't any of the countries conquered by Hitler refuse to go along with the Holocaust?

One did, in a big way: Denmark. On the northern border of Germany, Denmark shamefully but pragmatically surrendered to the Nazis with almost no resistance in 1940. Yet, three years later, when the Nazis tried to round up the country's 7,000 Jews, thousands of normal folks—taxi drivers, fishermen, doctors, nurses, bookstore owners, police officers, school kids, and more—banded together to form a far-ranging but secret conspiracy called the Freedom Council. Within days, they created a network of ad hoc safe houses, underground railroads, and a fleet of sympathetic fishermen. Within months, nearly every Danish Jew was safely smuggled out of the country to Sweden.

What did the "D" stand for in "D-Day"?

"Day." The term "D-Day" is typically used by the military to indicate the date of an attack without giving away the actual date. "H-Hour" is the hourly equivalent when discussing the time of an attack. "D-Day" as we know it became popularized during WWII when it was used to stand for the planned date of the Normandy invasion—June 6, 1944.

> **Did any country change sides in either of the World Wars?**
> Yes, Italy in 1943.

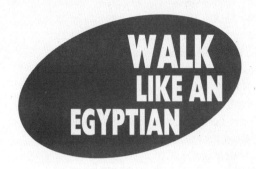

WALK LIKE AN EGYPTIAN

Ancient Egypt, the land of mystery, mysticism, intrigue, mummies, deserts, and pointlessly pointed monuments. Ever wonder what Cleopatra's beauty secrets were or how they got the brains out of mummies? Step forward and wonder no more.

HENCE CITIES NAMED ALEXANDRIA, CAIRO & MEMPHIS

America too has pyramids and mummies. Is there any chance that the ancient Egyptians were the first American explorers?

It's possible but unlikely. True, the New World pyramids were built from 1200 B.C. to the 1500s, slightly overlapping the time when Egyptians were doing the same thing (2700 B.C. to 1000 B.C.). However, the styles, building materials, shapes, and functions of the American pyramids were somewhat different from the Egyptian kind. Rather than pointy at the top, the American pyramids were more like layered cakes with a flat top. The Egyptian pyramids were designed as tombs and monuments; the American ones were used for ceremonies, like human sacrifices, and for military defense.

The oldest mummy in the world was found in Peru, dating from about 8000 B.C. Like the first Egyptian mummies, he was an accident, preserved naturally by dry desert air. However, here's a difference between the Egyptians and the prehistoric Native Americans: In about 2600 B.C., Egyptians began purposefully mummifying bodies; in contrast, the prehistoric Americans never deliberately preserved their dead.

> **What does "Nile" mean in ancient Egyptian?**
> "Water."

HOLY MOSES!

Did Israeli slaves build the pyramids?

No, despite what you might see in the movies, there's no evidence that Israelites worked on the pyramids. Archaeologists excavating the temporary villages and grave sites around the base of the pyramids have come to the conclusion that they were probably built by Egyptians as public works projects. They estimate that about 5,000 people lived and worked there at any one time, and that each pyramid took 20 to 40 years to build.

The Egyptians apparently worked in crews, perhaps centered around the villages they came from. There's evidence that they may have engaged in friendly competitions with other crews. On protected surfaces of blocks and hallways, archaeologists have found graffiti tagged with work-gang names like "Khufu's friends" and "the Drunks of Menkaura."

WHO'S THE PHAROAH'S ONE OF ALL?

Why did they name the condom brand "Ramses"?
Who was he, and did he actually use condoms?

The most famous guy by that name, Ramses II, was perhaps the greatest pharaoh of Egypt. He ruled for 67 years from 1279 to 1212 B.C. Despite the name, it's unlikely that condoms were part of Ramses' life since he fathered over 160 children. It was this virility that probably led the British-based company Durex—maker of the Sheik and the Ramses brand condoms—to name them after him.

Still, perhaps the old pharaohs should be given their due, even if condoms weren't apparently invented yet. As far as we know, Egyptian birth-control methods are the oldest in history. Two documents from about 1850 B.C. and 1550 B.C. detail numerous methods the Egyptians used. One of the more exotic and less appetizing perhaps worked as a spermicide: a mixture of crocodile dung and honey inserted into the vagina before intercourse.

MUMMY'S THE WORD

The Rosicrucian Museum in San Jose, California,
has a big display of Egyptian mummies. How did
they get so many? Aren't they hard to find?

Not as hard as you'd think. For nearly four thousand years, from 3100 B.C. to 649 A.D., Egyptians mummified their dead. That made for a lot of mummies lying about—about 500 million, according to best estimates. And that's just the humans; there were animals, too—cats, wild dogs, bulls, fish, birds, scorpions, insects, baboons, and crocodiles. One tomb that archaeologists uncovered, for example, contained more than a million mummified birds.

An old story I was reading mentioned a doctor prescribing "mummy powder." What the heck is mummy powder?

We'll get into that in a minute. First, though, let's look at the mummy situation from a 12th-century, Egyptian point of view. Finding mummies in your garden just about everywhere you sank a shovel could start getting on your nerves after a while, and it was pretty likely that this could happen with half a billion dead forebears buried all over the country's towns and villages.

Luckily, such problems sometimes suggest solutions. As Egyptians abandoned the old faith in favor of Islam, they no longer believed that destroying a mummified body would create problems for you in the next world. In a land without many trees or natural resources, people quickly discovered that mummies burned as well as coal, wood, or camel dung. It didn't take long before people began using mummies for cooking, heating, and powering their machinery.

Millions of mummies were burned to run the Egyptian railroads in the 19th century. World-traveler Mark Twain wrote about the practice, claiming that when he rode on an Egyptian train he heard an Egyptian engineer shout to his fireman, "Damn those plebians, they don't burn worth a cent. Pass me a king!"

In a time when the country had little to export but sand, Egyptians couldn't help but notice the morbid fascination mummies held for European travelers and adventurers. Suddenly, what was once an annoying, omnipresent liability— mummies, mummies everywhere—became an opportunity. In the 12th century, mummies became one of Egypt's biggest export products, and it stayed that way for more than 400 years.

This is where mummy powder comes in. Sometime in the 1100s, doctors in Europe and Asia began grinding up mummies and using the powder as a tea or poultice for its supposed health benefits. For a while it was considered a magical wonder drug and was prescribed for just about everything: nausea, epilepsy, migraines, coughs, bruises, fractures, paralysis, and as an antidote for poisoning. Not everybody thought the powder itself was good enough, however; the French insisted that a better medicine came from boiling the mummies and skimming off the mummy oil that rose to the top.

Supplies were plentiful and cheap. A Scot noted that the going rate for a pound of powder in the 17th century was about eight shillings. Besides the alleged health benefits, artists added it to their paints, figuring the magic in the mummies would keep the colors from fading over time. Finally, though, the famous 17th-century French surgeon Ambrose Peré helped drive a stake through the heart of the mummy powder craze when he wrote that "not only does this wretched drug do no good, but it causes great pain to the stomach, gives foul-smelling breath, and brings on serious vomiting." We can imagine.

So it was back to the drawing board for the Egyptian mummy exporters, but Europeans and Americans continued to provide a market for mummies. In the 1800s, it became a fad in the trendier parts of European society to invite friends over to unwrap a mummy. During a 19th-century rag shortage, a Canadian papermaker got the bright idea to buy some mummies, discard the bodies, and recycle the linens into food-wrap paper. Not a great idea: His paper was blamed for an outbreak of cholera shortly afterward.

If you unwrapped a mummy, how far would the cloth material go?
Almost half a mile.

What organ of the body was never removed when the Egyptians mummified it?
The heart was considered the seat of all thought, and it was always kept in the body.

MUMMY'S LITTLE HELPER

How did Egyptians make a mummy?

In Egypt, making a rudimentary mummy was pretty easy because of the dry heat: All you had to do was bury the corpse in sand for a few months. It would become so completely leatherized that it wouldn't rot. That lucky accident worked well enough for centuries and continued to work for regular folk for centuries thereafter. However, as time passed, Egypt's pharaohs and poo-bahs became more grandiose in their afterlife plans. They insisted on elaborate burial crypts filled with stuff, in the hope that the "can't take it with you" adage had some loopholes. The problem with the crypts was that the bodies didn't naturally mummify in the cool darkness; they rotted, and Egyptian pharaohs didn't want to be saddled with a stinking, moldy body in the next world. In response, the best minds of ancient Egypt worked out ways to mummify bodies that didn't require months of repose in hot desert sand.

According to the Greek historian Herodotus—writing in about 450 B.C.—there were three different processes for mummification, depending on what price you were willing to pay. The most expensive technique pulled out all the stops (and most of the organs)—the corpse's brain was liquefied with a specialized whisk shoved up the nostrils and then poured out through the nose, and all of the innards but the heart were removed through a side incision made with a sharp flint knife. Now-empty parts were filled with linen, sawdust, and mud, and the body was sprinkled with powdered natron, a naturally occurring salt compound that desiccated it in about 40 days. Afterward, the body was anointed with oils and herbs and wrapped in linens saturated with pitch or beeswax. The leftover organs were placed in nearby jars, and the mummy was put into a customized case. In the midrange method, the process was similar, but the organs weren't removed, and the body was merely injected with cedar oil before wrapping. Finally, the cheapest method was the functional equivalent of burying the body in hot sand: The body was simply dried out intact, without the secret herbs and spices or custom container.

How long did it take to turn a corpse into a mummy?

About 70 days.

WALK LIKE AN EGYPTIAN

How beautiful was Cleopatra?

Not as pretty as you'd imagine. A coin issued during her reign depicted her with straight hair, a hooked nose, and a pronounced chin. In fact, she looked disconcertingly like Robin Williams in drag.

So, perhaps Cleopatra had inner beauty. "Her beauty was by no means flawless," wrote the tactful historian Plutarch, adding that she had "irresistible charm" and a voice that was "beguilingly rich." That, and she had a kingdom the Romans had wanted to get their hands on for a long time. Still, she saved her kingdom for a while by becoming the lover of the two successive generals—Julius Caesar and Mark Antony—who had come to conquer Egypt, but were conquered by the lady's charms instead.

Was Cleopatra black?

There's absolutely no evidence to support the idea and much evidence to discount the possibility. Although many Egyptians *were* black, Cleopatra was not Egyptian. She descended from a line of Macedonian Greeks in a family so determined to avoid diluting the family blood that it practiced a severe form of incestuous interbreeding, in which brothers married sisters and fathers married daughters. (Cleopatra at 17, following the family ways, married her pesky 12-year-old brother. He was later slaughtered as he battled her for the throne, which should not be surprising to anyone who has had an older sister.)

PIZZA PIZZA

Did Cleopatra have children?

Yes. She had twins with Mark Antony. Before that, though, she had a son with Julius Caesar who she named Caesarion ("Little Caesar").

MY FACE IS MY CANVAS

Did Cleopatra use makeup?

Quite a bit of it, actually. She even used some of the pigments that artists of the age were also using, including lead, which probably shouldn't be placed on your face if you value your health and sanity. Still, if you want to inspire Roman hands, here are some of her secrets:

◆ Red ocher for cheek rouge

◆ Henna on your palms to give them a youthful glow

◆ A lead ore, called black galena, as an eyeliner and eyebrow pencil

◆ Lapis lazuli for a blue-black tint on your upper eyelid, and malachite (copper ore) for a green tint on your lower lid.

What kind of snake killed Cleopatra?

It might've been an especially poisonous asp called the Egyptian cobra. But it's not absolutely certain that a snake *did* kill Cleopatra. After her first Roman general, Julius Caesar, was assassinated, Cleopatra took up with Mark Antony, believing him to be on the fast track to Roman leadership. Unfortunately though, she chose the wrong horse, and when Octavius took over power, Cleopatra and Antony found it wise to flee Rome. He returned and tried to kiss up to Octavius by marrying his sister. However, this strategy backfired when Antony, upon realizing that he couldn't stay away from her charms, returned to Cleopatra in Egypt. An outraged Octavius took up arms against them both. Antony's dwindling army lost the battle outside Alexandria, and he returned to the palace in an uproar, not only incensed by his defeat but also by reports that Cleopatra had been secretly trying to make a deal with Octavius to ally with him and keep her throne.

Cleopatra hid in her mausoleum and sent a servant to tell Antony that she was dead. Aware that Octavius's army was battering at the gates and distraught about the whole damned situation, Antony stabbed himself. However, as he died slowly, he was informed that Cleopatra was still alive. Carried to her side, he died in her arms. Just as she was preparing to also stab herself, Octavius's army broke in, disarmed her, and kept her imprisoned (with her servants and the comforts of the palace) there in her mausoleum.

After several days, she had her servants dress her and give her the full beauty treatment. She wrote a note to Octavius asking to be buried with Antony. However, her death was not part of his plan—he was hoping to parade her naked through the streets of Rome to demonstrate his victory—so he rushed to her mausoleum, where he found a dead Queen lying regally on the bed and her two attendants lying on the floor. Two tiny marks were found on Cleopatra's arm. Although no snake was found in the sealed mausoleum, Octavius guessed that she might have killed herself with an asp hidden in a basket of figs that had been delivered earlier that day. However, it was also widely reported that she kept a dose of poison in a special hairpin she wore. We'll probably never know for sure.

What happened to Cleopatra's palace?

It still exists, but it's underwater. A fourth century earthquake accompanied by a tsunami caused the royal island of Antirhodos to sink into the sea. The ruins of the palace were rediscovered in the murky, sewage-filled Alexandria harbor in 1992.

EGYPTIAN ARTIFACTS ARE TOO, TOO UNCOMMON

Didn't King Tut's tomb have a curse?

Well, doesn't it seem pretty suspicious that, of all the people who opened the tomb in 1922, not a single one of them is still alive?

Seriously, though. The press in the 1920s made a big deal of a supposed "mummy's curse," claiming that it had taken 21 victims by 1935. However, in order to come up with that figure, they had to add in a whole lot of people who had nothing to do with the tomb. Journalists added in relatives, acquaintances, employees, or even (in one case) a relative of an employee to give credence to the alleged curse. Considering the ever-widening pool of friends, relatives, and acquaintances, it's actually surprising that there weren't more.

What did King Tut die of?

Tutankhamen, who died in 1325 B.C., was a minor king, serving for nine years from age nine to 18. Scientists believe he might have died from a blow to the head, though whether it was from an accident or an assassination is not known.

Were King Tut and Cleopatra related?

Well, maybe in the sense that we're all brothers and sisters and children of Mother Earth. Apart from that, they were separated by 1,300 years and came from completely different bloodlines. Tutankhamen was a native Egyptian king. Cleopatra was part of an interloper family that came from Greek Macedonia (in fact, although she was the last of her line, she was the first of them to actually learn the language of the Egyptian people).

Who found the Rosetta Stone?

A group of French engineers from Napoleon's army. In 1799, they were getting ready to demolish an ancient wall outside Rosetta, a city near Alexandria, Egypt. They stumbled upon a carved stone which, because it had the same message in three ancient languages, ended up becoming the key to translating Egyptian hieroglyphics.

It just goes to show that it's not always the archaeologists and explorers who make the most significant finds—in fact, it's often just some nobody who happens to be in the right place at the right time. For example, the discoverer of the Dead Sea Scrolls

was a simple herdsman looking for a lost goat.
Neanderthal Man was uncovered by a
group of German quarrymen in 1856.
And the ruins of the lost city of
Pompeii were discovered by a farmer
digging in his vineyard in 1748.

Ask!

Where can I
see a picture of the
Rosetta Stone?

·Emperor of Internet·

FEARLESS LEADERS

People seem to love to hear about madmen with power. From that crazy, horse-loving Caligula to the cruel impalings of the real Count Dracula (and a whole lot in between), here's the truth about some of our favorite fearless leaders.

STAKING OUT A PLACE IN HISTORY

How did they get the name "Dracula" from "Vlad the Impaler"?

His father, also named Vlad, was inducted into a secret Catholic organization called the Order of the Dragon, sworn to battle the

Ottoman Turks. When he became Prince of Walachia, his kingdom dubbed him *Dracul*, meaning, in Romanian, "The Dragon." When Vlad the Second came to power, he called himself *Dracula*, or "Son of the Dragon."

Ask! When Dracula impaled people where did the stake go and how long did the victim live?

What did young Vlad the Impaler want to be when he grew up?

Before becoming a principality ruler, military strategist, grand inquisitor, and sadist extraordinaire? He studied for the priesthood.

Wasn't Vlad the Impaler a Moslem?

Although young Vlad and his brother were bartered off to the Turkish Sultan as part of a peace treaty signed by his father, Vlad himself was by no means a follower of Islam. If anything, he fought hard against the Turks for most of his adult life, perhaps as a result of his bitterness from being held hostage by them during his childhood.

When Vlad was born in 1431, his family was Roman Catholic, but his father converted the family to Romanian Orthodox when he took the job of prince. His son Dracula converted back to Roman Catholicism sometime around 1476.

But even before that official point in his spiritual life, Vlad had already made his alliances clear. Vlad picked up that kicky little nickname *Kaziklu Bey* or "the Impaler" in 1462 when Pope Pius II ordered the heads of all European states to make war with the Ottomans under the lead of Mohammed II. Not many heads of state heeded the papal command except for Vlad. He put thousands of men, women, and children to battle, but beat the 250,000-man Ottoman army with terror, not manpower. Vlad impaled about 20,000 Turkish prisoners on long poles and lined them up along the stretch of road leading into the city, so that the Turks would see them as they marched toward it. Legend has it that Mohammed II saw the gruesome sight and commented, "Is it worth it?" He and his troops decided it wasn't and fled.

Ask! Can I tour Dracula's castle in Transylvania?

PATTON MEDICINE

Was General George Patton crazy?

Most would say he was eccentric, maybe worse. For starters, he had a long-term affair with his niece, who called him "Uncle Georgie." It's said he once urinated in a foxhole of another division commander during WWI, simply to show his disdain for what he called "passive defense." He was bloodthirsty and loved war for war's sake. While on the way into Germany, he was constantly taking his troops down the most dangerous routes. On one particular occasion, as the sky was lit with gunfire and bomb blasts, he threw his hands in the air and proclaimed to his troops: "Could anything be more magnificent? Compared to war, all other forms of life shrink to insignificance. God, how I love it!"

Patton also claimed to have a strong sense of déjà vu on many occasions, believing it to be a sign that he was reincarnated. He was certain that in his past incarnations, he had served as an infantryman under Napoleon, a prehistoric warrior, a Greek foot soldier fighting the Persians, a legionnaire with Julius Caesar in Gaul, and an English knight in the Hundred Years' War. He was disciplined for slapping two soldiers for being cowards who were being treated in army hospitals during the war.

Patton's unpredictability gave him an advantage over his enemies, making him invaluable to the allies during World War II. Even though Eisenhower refused to give the general free reign because he couldn't be trusted, he couldn't bring himself to let Patton go. For much of the war, Eisenhower had Patton stationed all over Europe, pretty much as a decoy, armed with inflatable trucks, a phantom army, and ships. Patton and his rubber troops were moved in darkness from one spot to another to make it look as though the D-Day attack would happen in Southern Norway. When the D-Day invasion finally did take place, the Germans were so convinced the event wouldn't happen without Patton and his troops that they held back military defenses, waiting for the "real" attack. France was stormed, and the rest is history.

FAMILY FUEHRER

Did Adolf Hitler have any brothers and sisters?

Yes, five siblings and two half-siblings. Hitler's father, Alois, had all of his children during his second and third marriages. The Hitler children were, in order, Alois Jr. and Angela by Alois's second wife; and Gustav, Ida, Otto, Edmund, Adolf, and Paula by his third wife. Of the eight kids, only Adolf, Paula, Angela, and Alois Jr. lived into adulthood.

Wasn't there incest in Adolf Hitler's family?

When Adolf's half sister, Angela, moved in and became his housekeeper, her daughter Geli was about 16. Hitler in many respects adopted Geli: He took her places, both educational and recreational, and he paid for her formal schooling. During this time, he also apparently fell in love with his teenage niece and refused to be separated from her. Ultimately, he moved her into his own apartment. But things were, apparently, less than idyllic. According to Geli, Hitler was "a monster." There are rumors that he sometimes whipped her with a bullwhip for pleasure. This may or may not be true, but the lovers' relationship was volatile, for sure, and it was well known that Hitler was intensely jealous of her. When Hitler discovered that Geli and his chauffeur were having an affair, he flew into a rage and fired the chauffeur. After a long and heated argument between Adolf and Geli one night, she picked up his pistol and killed herself. She was 23.

Ask! Was Hitler a vegetarian?

BEFORE THEY WERE FAMOUS

What did Benito Mussolini do before he became a fascist dictator?

He was editor of a couple of political newspapers, including one for the Socialist Party. When he jumped ship and became a Nationalist, he started a different paper. He then joined the army before rising through the ranks—on his way to becoming Il Duce. However, before he was *any* of these things, he was a school teacher. Any school kid will tell you that that makes perfect sense.

What did Joseph Stalin do before becoming a militant dictator?

He studied for the priesthood but was expelled from the seminary in 1899 and joined the Communist Party.

CLARK KENT HAD THE SAME NAME

Was "Joseph" Stalin's real name?

Iosif Dzhugashvili was his given name (Iosif is "Joseph" in Russian). He was known to his parents, however, as "Soso." He adopted the name Stalin, meaning "man of steel," sometime around 1912, right after he was elected to the Communist Party's Central Committee.

Which World War II leader was on the cover of Time *magazine the most?*

Joseph Stalin.

What did Stalin look like?

According to a physical description the police circulated when he was a known revolutionary troublemaker, he was only five feet, four inches tall. The notice goes on, painting a less-than-attractive picture:

- Soft voice
- Birthmark on left ear
- Sunken, hazel eyes
- Pockmarked face
- Withered left arm
- Second and third toes on left foot grown together
- Thick, black hair and mustache (but no beard)

GEE! MEN!

Did J. Edgar Hoover ever date?

In a fashion, he did. He "kept company" with some women. One was Lela Rogers (actress Ginger Rogers's mother and an extreme right winger). He also claimed to have had a relationship with Dorothy Lamour. Hoover certainly wanted the public to *believe* he had relationships with these women. Whether they were anything more than platonic is unknown, and in some circles, considered highly doubtful. He did, however, have a male companion named Clyde Tolson. The two were inseparable for 44 years—living together, vacationing together, dressing alike, and even buried side by side. The couple caused much gossip in those homophobic times.

HUN, I'M HOME!

Did Genghis Khan and Attila the Hun ever fight each other?

Not in this world. Although both were considered ruthless scourges of civilization and so had much in common, they were separated by thousands of miles. That, and more than seven centuries. Attila terrorized Europe in the fifth century; Genghis terrorized China in the 12th and 13th.

> **Where did the Huns come from geographically?**
> Hungary.

Whose lame-brain idea was it to put Venice on islands? Or did they know they were building a tourist trap?

In a strange way, you can give backhanded credit to Attila the Hun, back in the fifth century. Tired of being raided by his gang of ruffians, the residents of several Italian towns decided to pack up their stuff and relocate to a series of islands just off the coast. They figured, correctly, that they'd be safe—Huns pretty much lived on horseback and weren't at all keen on boatbuilding. As much of the rest of Europe was looted and pillaged, Venice stayed safe and became a center of worldwide trade.

MAKE WAR, NOT LOVE

Did Attila the Hun die in battle?

No, in bed on his wedding night. After a night of passion, he died of a fatal nosebleed.

Which conqueror captured the most land in history?

Genghis Kahn wins, hands down, with an estimated total of 4,860,000 square miles. That's twice as much land as conquered by the runner up, Alexander the Great.

How much land did Napoleon conquer?

720,000 square miles.

FRENCH KISS-OFF

Was Napoleon executed after being deposed as leader of France?

No. He tried unsuccessfully to officially step down and have his son put on the throne. But when that idea was rejected, he abdicated voluntarily anyway and was exiled to the island of Elba in the Mediterranean. His wife and only child were sent to live with his father-in-law—the emperor of Austria—and he never saw them again. He did, however, manage to escape Elba. In 1815, he returned to France, rallied the troops, and marched on to Paris. He quickly tried to make peace with his former enemies but was refused. When pushed to battle, he was defeated by the British at the battle of Waterloo. Despite his popularity back home, Britain and its allies exiled him once more—this time for good—to the island of St. Helena in the South Atlantic Ocean, where he died of stomach cancer six years later.

MMMMM! FROG LEGS

Is it true that Napoleon and Josephine never consummated their marriage?

Not true at all. By all accounts, they had a very passionate relationship. Still, there was a painful moment on their wedding night when man's best friend became anything but. They were in bed making love when suddenly Napolean cried out. Josephine thought he was in the throes of passion, but it wasn't the love bug that was biting him. It was her dog. Apparently thinking his mistress was being attacked, the dog had jumped onto the bed and bit Napoleon on the leg. "All night the disappointed Josephine had to put compresses on her invalid's wound," wrote biographer M. de Ravine. "He huddled in the bed, moaning loudly that he was dying of rabies."

Wasn't Napoleon really short?

He was about the same height as the average Frenchman at the time; however, he was shorter than most leaders of his day and certainly shorter than most men today. He stood at five feet, two inches tall. This earned him the nickname *Petit Caporal* or "the Little Corporal."

LEFT BOOT, RIGHT BOOT—BOOT, BOOT, BOOT

Where does Caligula fit into the Roman emperor lineup?

Gaius Caesar Augustus Germanicus, nicknamed Caligula, was the third Roman emperor after Augustus and Tiberius. His name meant "Little Boots" in Latin. Like so many parents since, his parents thought he looked cute as a child dressed in a soldier's uniform, and his nickname stuck. His reign was short—only 3 years, 10 months. Following a brief and unknown illness early in his reign, Caligula went insane, killing most of his relatives, having people tortured while he dined, and naming his horse a consul. The Praetorian Guard secretly plotted and assassinated him in 41 A.D., when he was 28 years old.

YOU LIKE "PET TOSSER" BETTER?

Why was Czar Ivan called "Terrible"?

The first czar of Russia, crowned in 1547 at the age of 17, was dubbed terrible because he really was. His entire rule was tainted with senseless, brutal acts against his countrymen. In his childhood, Ivan IV liked tossing cats and dogs off ramparts just to see what would happen. During his reign he had thousands of people put to death, some in the most horrible of ways (Ivan liked reenacting biblical scenes of hell as part of an execution). It's said he put out the eyes of his own architect because, after he had designed the Kremlin, Ivan didn't want him building anything as beautiful anywhere else. He even beat his eldest son to death in a fit of rage. This act of cruelty was the last straw for Ivan's poor psyche. He had earlier lost his wife, Anastasia—whom, by all indications, he was totally devoted to—and now he was responsible for killing his own heir. Out of deep guilt and sorrow, Ivan paid for prayers to be said for all of those whom he'd killed over the years, forgave them all posthumously, and was rechristened as a monk named Jonah. He was buried in monk's clothing, but left a legacy of cruelty that haunts him to this day. However, in his own country of Russia, he's a national hero for bringing together the principalities of Russia under one crown.

SWEET LAND OF LIBERTY

They came from far and wide searching for gold, territory, escape, and freedom. What they found was a harsh voyage, difficult weather, and a land so vast it couldn't be imagined. From big hats and brass buckles to creaking sea voyages, we present the beginnings of what we now call the United States.

HEAD COUNT

How many natives were in the Americas before Europeans arrived?

Estimates vary from 8 to 16 million.

How many Native Americans were in what is now the United States at the beginning of the 20th century?

Fewer than 250,000.

Where was the first European colony in America?

That first documented European colony in America would have to be the Viking colony, dating from about 1000 A.D. in what is now northern Newfoundland. Excavations at a location called L'Anse aux Meadows bear artifacts from Greenland at around this time period, and ancient manuscripts from Greenland speak of a country full of grapevines that the Vikings (under the leadership of Erik the Red's son, Leif Eriksson) named *Vinland*. Other excavations farther north and south hint that the Vikings may have explored the eastern coast of the American continent in great depth. Historians guess that the natives and weather conditions may have cut short the first European colonies in the new world.

BORN IN THE U.S.A.

Who was the very first English person to be born in the New World?

On August 18, 1587—just days after the first colonists had arrived in Roanoke—John White's daughter gave birth to what most consider to be the very first English person born on American soil. They named the baby girl Virginia in honor of the virgin queen, Elizabeth I. The colony was named for the same reason.

GONE COUNTRY

Does anyone actually know whatever happened to the lost colony of Roanoke?

No. However, there are speculations based on some scant evidence. Briefly, the group of about a hundred English men, women, and children came to Roanoke under the leadership of a man named John White in 1587, looking to set up a permanent residence. Things seemed happy enough. However, come the summer of 1589, after the group had weathered a couple of hard winters, White decided he needed to return to England for more supplies for the little colony. After loading up with stuff in England, White started home but was delayed due to England's hostility with Spain. He finally made it back to Roanoke, but it was at least a year later. What he found waiting for him (or not!) is the source of great controversy. The village stood as he remembered it—completely intact—however, there wasn't a soul to be found in or around it. The entire colony had simply vanished, leaving but one clue: Carved into a tree was the word "Croatan," the name of a group of Native Americans that lived nearby.

No one ever heard from any of the members of the Roanoke colony again. News of the mystery was downplayed in England for fear it would scare potential settlers away from continuing to move to the new world.

What about the Croatans? Did they kill or enslave the English settlers?

It was discovered years later that a group of Native Americans calling themselves Croatans inhabited the hills of North Carolina and still do to this day. Some of these tribesmen, although very much of Native American culture, bore English names; offering, perhaps, the answer to the eventual fate of the Roanoke colonists. Some historians believe they sought food and shelter from the Native American tribe, leaving John White the message so he could follow.

NOT EXACTLY THE DISNEY VERSION

What was Pocahontas's English name?

Her Indian name, Pocahontas, meant *playful one*. When she was baptized as a Christian, she was given the name Rebecca.

> **Did Pocahontas marry John Smith?**
> No, John Rolfe.

How and when did Pocahontas die?

A year after sailing to London to help raise funds for the English colonists in Virginia, she died of smallpox in 1617. Her young son, Thomas, was raised and educated in England, later returning to Virginia to live as an adult.

Ask! Where can I see a portrait of Pocahontas?

BASKING IN REFLECTED GLORY

How old was Pocahontas when she saved John Smith's life?

Theoretically, she would've been 12; however, it's somewhat questionable that the incident ever took place. In an earlier book, John Smith never mentioned the incident. It was only after Pocahontas gained fame and adoration in England as an Indian "princess" that Smith suddenly began telling the story about the time she supposedly got her father to spare his life.

APRIL SHOWERS

Where in England did the Pilgrims come from?

They'd lived in Holland for years to escape English religious persecution. They only returned to Southampton, England, to find ships to take them across to America. Two ships were hired, the *Mayflower* and the *Speedwell,* but the Speedwell had numerous problems almost from the moment they departed.

They stopped off in Dartmouth and Plymouth for repairs before dumping the *Speedwell,* reorganizing their traveling group and continuing with just the *Mayflower* on September 16, 1620. As a result, their departure point is usually considered Plymouth, England.

Was the Mayflower *built especially for the famous Pilgrim voyage to America?*

No. Ships made just for carrying passengers weren't in existence at the time. Records are sketchy, but the ship that most likely carried the Pilgrims was built around 1606 as a merchant ship that carried goods around the main ports of Europe. Before and after the famous New World voyage, the *Mayflower* carried hemp, cloth, hats, Spanish salt, hops, vinegar, tar, pine planks, and herring. She was known as a "sweet ship," meaning she also carried a lot of wine. The sticky, sweet smell of spilled port permeated the enclosed areas of the ship's hold.

How did the Pilgrims pay for their voyage to America?

They had a corporate sponsor. After King James I refused to give the Pilgrims a charter to start a colony, the London Virginia Company, a group of merchants with financial interest in the American colonies, was more than happy to help the Pilgrims make their journey and set up a colony across the Atlantic—for a price. That price was seven years of sweat and labor. Basically, the Pilgrims became indentured servants for the first seven years in America in order to complete their voyage. Any profits they made were to be sent to the London Virginia Company back home. At the end of the indentured period, the Pilgrims would be free to keep whatever profit they made from their businesses.

That was the arrangement. However, a dispute with a representative from the London Virginia Company took place on the docks of Southampton prior to their departure, causing the contract to be voided. With the Pilgrims' funds dwindling down to zero, they had to sell some of their butter to pay dock fees. The voyaging group also decided to take on extra passengers for the trip to help further defray expenses. This led to the division among the 102 *Mayflower* passengers of "strangers" and "saints": the saints being the 41 Pilgrim separatists, and the strangers being regular folk. The division disappeared once the travelers landed and began to set up their colony. The Mayflower Contract bound each person—Pilgrim or not—to work for the well-being of the group as a whole.

Who captained the Mayflower?

John Smith of Pocahontas fame was supposed to lead the way, but the Pilgrims couldn't afford his fees. Instead, they bought a book from him that included a map of the new region. So they went without the hired help of a captain. But this was a technicality. The ship's master, Christopher Jones, had been sailing with the *Mayflower* for years, knew the ins and outs of maneuvering her, and also had experience with this particular route. The Pilgrims, whether they realized it or not, were in good hands on the voyage.

Was the Mayflower *a small, rickety old ship?*

You would think so by reading the Pilgrims' accounts of the voyage. However, they weren't familiar with the nautical life, so they were not accustomed to the hardships. Thinking their lives were always in constant danger, their journals reflect a much more harrowing journey than it probably seemed to the more experienced crew and passengers. As to size, the *Mayflower* was actually pretty big. We know she was referred to as an "180-tun" ship. A tun is a large barrel or cask, able to carry about 265 gallons. That meant that the *Mayflower* could transport 180 full barrels in the hold area of the ship. Based on this, historians estimate that the ship had a length of about 90 feet.

Although the landlubber Pilgrims were convinced that the *Mayflower* was falling apart, in actuality she was unusually seaworthy. For 12 years prior she'd been sailing the North seas— the roughest sailing seas in the world—between Spain, France, the Scandinavian countries, and probably Italy as well. A main beam did crack during a storm on the voyage, but the Pilgrims were traveling at one of the worst times of the year for storms, and the ship weathered even that well enough. The fact is that the *Mayflower* was a tough ship that managed to survive storm after storm on the crossing, making the voyage in good time. On her return trip in the following spring, traveling with the prevailing winds, she made the trip in less than half the time it took to initially get across the Atlantic: 31 days.

Ask!
Where can I learn more about the Mayflower II?

Did any animals make the Mayflower *voyage in 1620?*

Although there was no livestock on board, there probably was the usual cat or two to keep the rat populations in check. We also know that at least two passengers brought pet dogs, a mastiff and a spaniel used to hunt during the first winter months in America. Most historians believe there were surely more, but these two were the only ones mentioned in journals.

How long did the voyage take to get to New England on the Mayflower?

It took the *Mayflower* 66 days to get from England to Cape Cod. That meant the boat was traveling at about two miles per hour throughout the trip, which isn't too bad considering the strong Gulf Stream and the stormy weather during the September/October season. One hundred years later, the fastest clippers were making the exact same voyage going no faster than about three miles per hour.

> **How many Pilgrims survived the first winter in America?**
> Fewer than 50.

How much was the Mayflower appraised for at the end of her sailing years?

One hundred twenty-eight English pounds and 12 shillings.

NOT WELL SUITED FOR THE TIMES

Why did the Pilgrims wear those goofy hats and buckles?

Actually, their portrayal as fashion victims is a terrible injustice that's been done to the poor Pilgrims. It's all a lie: They never wore clothes like that. In reality, Pilgrims dressed as others of the day dressed, in various colors of clothing that would never have stood out on the streets of England.

So how did it happen that pilgrims came to be seen this way? The holiday of Thanksgiving became all the rage during 19th-century America—certainly more popular and more practiced than ever before or since. During this time, artists began to render their interpretations of what these first colonists might have looked like: old fashioned, prim, and sternly proper. Before anyone knew it, a completely false image had emerged as an American icon: bearded men with tall hats; women, men, and children dressed in stark black and white; high-tongued shoes and large bulky buckles. It was simply a look that Americans in the 1800s decided to foist upon its early settlers.

Ask! Where can I see pictures of the clothing from the early 1600s?

PAIN DOWN UNDER

How come the British started shipping their worst criminals to Australia?

Because America won the Revolution. After 1780, the British could no longer use their penal colonies in Maryland, Georgia, and Virginia and had to find another place. Sending criminals far away from home was an extreme punishment only reserved for the worst offenders, but it meant avoiding the costs of building new jails and feeding the prisoners. So it didn't take long for Australia to become Britain's penal colony of choice.

EVER-EXPANDING COUNTRY

Who got taken when the Dutch bought Manhattan from the Indians for $24 worth of trinkets?

More than a century ago, the price was estimated to be about $24, but based on the recent price of silver, it would be more like $100 in today's money. Still, it's not surprising that we expect that somebody must've gotten ripped off—probably the Indians, considering the price. That expectation is no doubt heightened by the fact that New York City has the long-held reputation for being a place full of grifters and con artists.

Let's look at it from the points of view of the participants. First of all, did the Dutch deliberately underpay when they paid sixty guilders worth of cloth, beads, hatchets, and other goods for the land? Seeing what Manhattan's become now, it's easy to say they snookered the Indians, but at the time, Manhattan was swampy and not that promising. Furthermore, it was a place where land was plentiful, at a time when most settlers didn't even bother to pay *anything* for the land they settled, so maybe it was a fair deal for the Indians.

In fact, maybe it was *more* than fair. Upon further inspection of the situation, the Dutch were probably sold the equivalent of the Brooklyn Bridge. Some historians believe that the tribe Peter Minuit paid—the Canarsies—actually lived on Long Island and just happened to be passing through Manhattan on a trading expedition. In which case, they sold land that they didn't even own. As a result, the white guys later had to buy part of the island all over again from the tribes who actually lived there. Still, they were better off than some—the Raritan tribe sold Staten Island to various groups of settlers no less than six times.

So did the Dutch make a good investment? Taking the price they paid in 1626 and comparing it with the total value of land now, economists estimate that the original investment has earned about 5.3% annual appreciation. Not bad, but no great shakes. Maybe they should've put their money into Atlantic City.

In today's dollars, how much did the U.S. pay France for the Louisiana Purchase?

The $15 million paid back then is the equivalent of just under $171 million dollars in today's money—a steal even now. In 1803, the U.S. got Arkansas, Iowa, Minnesota west of the Mississippi River, North Dakota, South Dakota, Missouri, Nebraska, nearly all of Kansas, the portions of Montana, Wyoming, and Colorado east of the Rocky Mountains, Oklahoma, the parts of Louisiana that were west of the Mississippi River, and the city of New Orleans. Of the money paid, only about $11 million went directly to the French government at that time; the rest was paid to residents who had filed claims against France for selling what was their formerly French property. The U.S. agreed to pay these claims for France as part of the deal.

INVENTIONS, EXPLORERS, & DISCOVERIES

Ever wonder about early uses for cabbage or who the heck thought up the Chihuahua? You're not alone. From the flawed human characters who led the way to brave new worlds, to the weird icons behind everyday inventions, "Ask Jeeves" presents discoveries and inventions and those who made them possible.

WIPING CLEAN THE ANNALS OF HISTORY

When was toilet paper first used, and what did they use before?

The Chinese were the first to use such paper by recycling paper that had already been used for other purposes. How do we know this? Because a court official wrote in 589 A.D. that he was careful not to use documents with "quotations from the great writers." Before that? Well, there were leaves, rocks, or whatever was available. The Romans were a little more civilized; they used a sponge attached to a stick. Toilet paper as we know it wasn't invented until 1879 by an Englishman named Walter Alcock.

TURNING UP THE VOLUMES

Which came first, books or libraries?

Libraries came first. Early Egyptian libraries lent out literature that came pressed and fired into clay tablets.

Who wrote the first encyclopedia?

The Chinese did in about 220 A.D. It was called *The Emperor's Mirror,* and included historical texts, biographies, and literary anthologies. No copies survived. The next known extensive encyclopedic work came from Spain and was titled *Etymologiae.* Saint Isidore of Seville is credited with writing it sometime between the sixth and seventh century. The 20-volume tome included entries in history, mathematics, agriculture, war, medicine, art, and theology. As a result of this early data collecting, the Vatican has made Isidore the patron saint of school children, computer programmers, and the Internet.

Ask! Where can I find a prayer to St. Isidore on the Internet?

SOMETHING NEW UNDER THE SUN

Who invented sunscreen?

Egyptian shepherds made sunscreen from crushed castor beans in 7800 B.C.

Did the Egyptians invent anesthetics?

Sort of. Before surgery, ancient Egyptian doctors put their patients under by hitting them on the head with a wooden hammer. Surprisingly, none were sued, despite this mallet-practice.

"AND THEY CALLED IT PUPPY GLO-O-O-VES . . ."

Where did the Chihuahua come from, and why would anybody purposely breed such a ridiculously small dog?

Maybe as hand warmers. The forebears of Chihuahuas were first developed by the Toltecs, a wandering Central American tribe. When the Aztecs conquered the Toltecs, they also won the Toltec dog, which they crossbred with other small dogs to get even smaller dogs (in fact, the Chihuahua is the world's smallest dog). Why the Aztecs wanted such a small dog is still a matter of speculation. Evidence and anecdote suggest that the royal Aztecs used the small dogs as pets and even as hand warmers in drafty palaces. Aztec priests sacrificed them to the gods and cremated them with dead people to act as protection against evil spirits and as faithful guides to the Other World. The common people? They cherished Chihuahuas as household pets—and food.

What "Bell" is Taco Bell referring to? A mission bell? The Liberty Bell?

Would you believe a guy named Glen Bell? The "Bell" in Taco Bell is the founder's last name. The whole mission bell motif was a fortunate by-product, especially considering that the restaurant's original logo was a Mexican taking a siesta under a sombrero.

A FORD IN YOUR FUTURE?

Jeeves, my wife insists that Henry Ford, the father of the Model T, was a Nazi. Say it ain't so!

Henry Ford was a renowned anti-Semite who was highly regarded by Hitler and the Nazis, not only for his car-making abilities but for his politics as well.

You don't see much of this side of Ford early on, when he paid high wages and provided fair working conditions for blacks and other minorities. Granted, he didn't play fair with his female workers (believing they were temporary and wouldn't prove useful to him in the long term), but at the onset of WWI, he was paying blacks equal wages and promoting them to supervisory positions within his company—a rare exception back then. And after the war, a quarter of his workforce was made up of people with disabilities long before any laws dictated fair hiring practices.

It was after Ford got fame and money that his anti-Semetic views surfaced. His newspaper, *The Dearborn Independent,* made it clear in issue after issue how Ford felt about Jews. Using his paper to express his opinions about a worldwide Jewish conspiracy against gentiles earned him a unique honor: He's the only American Hitler praised in his infamous *Mein Kampf.* Hitler reportedly lifted whole sections of editorials out of Ford's *Dearborn Independent* and used them in his book. Rumors that Ford provided direct financial aid to the Nazis in their early years have never been definitively proved or disproved.

Besides soy beans, what other plants did Henry Ford grow for experimentation?

Would you believe dope? In his experimental gardens Ford grew marijuana in the hopes of figuring out a way to make plastic from it. Apparently nothing, aside from a distinct feeling of relaxation, came of this youthful experimentation. And strangely, there's nothing that mentions these efforts at the Ford history museum.

AUTOBIOGRAPHIES

Where did Henry Ford get the name of his biggest bomb, the Edsel?

It was actually Henry Ford II, the grandson of the famous Henry Ford, who named the Edsel after his dad. The name Edsel is a Germanic derivation of the name Atilla, but it's unlikely that Ford executives meant to honor the ruthless Hun when they named it. When Edsel Ford died in 1943, he willed all of his Ford stock to the Ford Foundation.

What is the diesel in diesel fuel?

That would be Rudolf Diesel. He's not actually in the fuel, mind you, except in spirit. The German inventor developed the diesel engine back in 1890.

Who's responsible for the Volkswagen Beetle?

Originally? Ferdinand Porsche, the designer of the speedy roadster, also designed the Bug for the government-owned Volkswagen car company. Adolf Hitler financed it.

OOPS! I DID IT AGAIN

So the key and kite thing didn't electrocute Ben Franklin. Did he ever fully understand the potentially fatal power of electricity?

He certainly did. As a matter of fact, in another of his experiments, he once knocked himself temporarily senseless. At the time, he was trying to electrocute a turkey and nearly killed two birds with one thunderbolt. Here's part of his account to a colleague:

> I have lately made an experiment that I desire never to repeat. Two nights ago, being about to kill a turkey by the shock from two large glass jars, containing as much electrical fire as forty common phials, I inadvertently took the whole through my own arms and body, by receiving the fire from the united top wires with one hand, while the other held a chain connected with the outside of both jars.

Franklin goes on to physically describe the event and its sensations and effects. He ends with this embarrassed plea:

> *You may communicate this to Governor Bowdoin as a caution to him, but do not make it more public, for I am ashamed to have been guilty of so notorious a blunder; a match for that of the Irishman whom my sister told me of, who, to divert his wife, poured the bottle of gun powder on the live coal; or that of the other, who, being about to steal powder, made a hole in the cask with a hot iron.*

What experiment was Thomas Edison attempting to do as a child when he burned his father's barn down?

Merely attempting to start a fire, apparently. Al, as he was called throughout his childhood, claimed he started it deliberately, "just to see what it would do." Good kid, that Al, but keep an eye on him.

TUBULAR, DUDE!

What did Philo T. Farnsworth, the inventor of television, do before becoming an inventor?

Not much. When Farnsworth sketched his idea for a television for the first time in 1922, it was for a science project, and it was drawn on a high school blackboard in Utah. At the time, he was a 14-year-old farm boy, yet to discover college and the world beyond. That sketch would prove pivotal in television history, in more ways than just the obvious. Years later, Farnsworth would have to battle the radio giant RCA over rights to his patent. During litigation, that blackboard sketch and his high school science teacher became crucial evidence in court and made Farnsworth the first independent inventor to ever win a royalty-paying patent license from RCA.

Ask! *Why is there no broadcast Channel 1 on TV?*

TO LEAVE A MESSAGE FOR WATSON, PRESS "2"

Wasn't Alexander Graham Bell a Bostonian?

Sort of. He was born in Edinburgh, Scotland, but immigrated to the U.S. in 1871, spending most of his work time in Boston. But he spent his summers at Cape Breton Island in Nova Scotia, Canada, where he had a summer home.

Why did Alexander Graham Bell work with sound for the deaf? Was he deaf?

He wasn't deaf, but his mother was. Also, his father and grandfather were both speech experts. It was his work with electronically transmitted vowel sounds for the hearing-impaired that ultimately led to the invention of the telephone. Ironically, he considered the phone a mere trifle and expected that posterity would remember him for his pioneering work with the deaf.

Did Alexander Graham Bell invent other things besides the telephone?

Certainly. He was the inventor of the hydrofoil boat, a man-carrying kite, the aileron (a moveable part of an airplane wing that helps control rolling), and the landing/take-off airplane tricycle gear. He was also a cofounder of the National Geographic Society.

Bell also inadvertently invented a land-mine detector. When President Garfield was shot, Alexander Graham Bell showed up with a metal-detector contraption, hoping to locate the site of the bullet. Unfortunately, in an era when sanitation was poorly understood, President Garfield's health slowly declined from infections introduced by unsterile fingers and instruments being shoved into his bullet wound. Because Bell's invention was able to detect the bullet within the body the principle was later adapted into the land-mine detector. Unfortunately, it wasn't able to save the president.

HOME IMPROVEMENTS

When did the Venetians invent their famous slatted window blinds?

They didn't. It was British designer, Edward Beran, who, in 1769, enclosed adjustable wooden slats into a frame in order to regulate the amount of light coming into a room. They became known as Venetian blinds as a marketing ploy because Italian furnishings were considered very sophisticated in England at the time.

Who invented hammocks?

Caribbean natives. Columbus saw them lounging around in hammocks on his first trip to the New World. The name comes from the hamack tree, the bark of which was woven to make the comfy portable beds.

Who invented the pedal trash can?

Dr. Lillian Gilbreth, who also invented the electric mixer. She was a pioneering efficiency expert and, incidentally, was also the mother in the book *Cheaper by the Dozen,* written by two of her 12 children.

A BILLION CHINESE CAN'T BE WRONG

Blech! Who invented cabbage?

Cabbage, that smooth and crunchy source of vitamin C, seems to have been with us since time began. Evidence of its use dates back to more than 4,000 years ago in China. Ancient scrolls reveal that cabbage was actually used as a remedy for baldness in men—yet another condition that's been with us since the dawn of time.

IS THERE A DOCTOR IN THE HUT?

Who said "Dr. Livingstone, I presume?" and why?

Henry Morton Stanley said it. Stanley was a Welsh adventurer in the 19th century who, prior to his fame, had become a naturalized American citizen and fought in the American Civil

War. He had also been a member of the merchant marines, had fought with the British against the Ethiopian king, Theodore II, and had trekked West to report for the *New York Herald* on the American expansion into the frontier. He earned a reputation as an adventurer, chasing stories around the globe for newspaper editors. As a result, the *New York Herald* commissioned him once again in 1869 to "go find Livingstone!" in Africa.

Dr. David Livingstone, a Scottish missionary and explorer, had left for Africa some three years earlier searching for the source of the Nile River. He hadn't been heard from since that time. The world was curious about what had happened to him. Was he dead? Was he lost? Did he decide to "go native" and never come back? Stanley set out to retrace his steps.

Stanley left the island of Zanzibar on March 21, 1871, with about 2,000 men, and headed into the interior of Africa. On November 10, his party came across an encampment at Lake Tanganyika. When a weak and sickly doctor emerged from his tent, Stanley asked him, "Dr. Livingstone, I presume?" The whole story was put into his *New York Herald* article. The phrase traveled the globe, becoming part of modern history.

Stanley resupplied Livingstone and nursed him back to health. The two then explored the northern end of Lake Tanganyika together before Stanley headed back home in 1872, leaving Livingstone to continue on with his exploration. Two years later, when Livingstone died, Henry Stanley packed up and headed back to Africa to continue where Livingstone left off, still searching for the source of the Nile.

HEADS, YOU LOSE

Did Sir Walter Raleigh die while exploring?

No. And despite his role in first bringing tobacco home to Britain from the New World, he didn't die of smoking-related diseases, either. In fact, he was beheaded. He had been a favorite of Queen Elizabeth I, but Elizabeth died, and the crown was passed to her cousin, James I, who didn't share Elizabeth's fondness for the world explorer. He imprisoned Raleigh for treason for 12 years. After being released, Raleigh again angered the king by attacking and pillaging Spanish settlements in South America, and he was sentenced to death. On the morning of his death, he wrote a sweet letter to his wife and joked with the executioner about his ax: "Dost thou think that I am afraid of it? This is that that will cure all sorrows." His body was buried in London, but his head was not. His wife had it embalmed and kept it in a red leather bag until her death 29 years later.

YOU'RE A VIKING? NORWAY!

How did Erik the Red end up in Greenland?

He was running out of places to go. He had been exiled from Iceland for murder, so he decided to see what was out there beyond the icy horizon.

Erik Thorvaldson, called "the Red" because of the color of his hair, was born in Norway, but when he was about 10 years old his father was exiled for manslaughter. Father and son ended up in Iceland. When Erik grew up, he followed his father's bad example and killed a couple of people himself, and so was exiled from Iceland for three years. During his exile, Erik headed west to look for land that another Norse explorer, Gunnbjorn Ulfsson, had spotted about 80 years earlier. Erik reached a new land and decided that it might be even better than Iceland, if such a thing were possible. At least it was large and uninhabited, which decreased the chances that he'd run into someone who needed killin' again.

After his three years of exile were up, Erik went back to Iceland to convince people to join him in making a new settlement. No fool he, he called the land "Greenland" as a bit of consumer fraud to make the new land sound like it was more than just another godforsaken mass of rocks and ice. In about 985, Erik sailed to Greenland again, this time accompanied by 25 ships full of colonists and supplies. By the time they had navigated the icy waters, the fleet was down to 14 ships. Still, the rough trip proved a good incentive for the

450 people who actually made it to stay. To avoid overcrowding, they founded two settlements 300 miles apart. Despite communication problems inherent in the days before e-mail, telephones, and Federal Express, Erik was a leader in both communities.

Strangely enough, it didn't take long for Erik to start feeling like civilization was closing in on him again. In the midst of a 40-something midlife crisis, he started planning another expedition west to look for even more land. On the way to his ship on launch day, though, he fell off his horse. Taking it as an omen from the gods, he decided to go awandering no more. But fear not: The days of roving Vikings weren't over yet. Just as Erik had followed the path of his own father, Lief, Erik's son, followed Erik's unfinished path. Around 1002, Leif Eriksson headed west and landed someplace in North America—most likely Newfoundland, but it's also quite possible that he got as far south as Massachusetts Bay.

Did Viking explorer Leif Eriksson have any brothers?

He had two: Thorvald and Thorstein. He also had a sister named Freydis.

LOST IN THE TRANSLATION

How did Canada get its name?

From the Iroquois word "Kanata," meaning "village." Explorer Jacques Cartier, for lack of a better name, called the whole region "Canada"—his interpretation of the Iroquois term—and it stuck.

SPACE CASES

Was it John Glenn or Alan Shepard who said, "That's one small step for a man, one giant leap for mankind"?

Neither, and remember next time: It was Neil Armstrong.

THE 600-MILE HIGH CLUB

Has anyone had sex in space?

Not that we know of, but apparently, it's become a very hot
subject. Rumors, speculations, and outright hoaxes can be found
all over the Internet. One of them claims that the first woman in
space, a Russian cosmonaut named Svetlana Savitskaya, had
sex with one of her two male cotravelers back in 1982. Another,
written to look like it was a government document, purports
that NASA did tests to try out different sexual positions using a
variety of harnesses, grips, and Velcro. There was also
speculation about the first married couple to go into space.
These and other sexual rumors were never supported by
evidence and were denied across the board by the fellow crew
members, the guys who watched the live cams, and the
principals themselves. Add the privacy issue as a formidable
obstacle: Most missions consist of 5 to 7 people in a space that's
about the size of a school bus.

On the other hand, the answer might also depend on what
you mean by sex. We've been talking about two-person sex
here. Although nobody's willing to talk about it much,
masturbation has probably occurred. In fact, according to
Apollo 11 astronaut Michael Collins, mission doctors advised
them to engage in the practice as a way of preventing infections
of the prostate gland.

HEY, YOU WITH THE FEATHERS! WHICH WAY TO NANKING?

How many times did Columbus come to the New World?

Columbus voyaged to the New World on four different occasions,
all of them financed by Isabella and Ferdinand, the king and
queen of Spain. On his first voyage, he "discovered" San
Salvadore, Cuba, the Dominican Republic, and Haiti. On his
second trip, he landed on the islands of Dominica, Jamaica, and
Guadeloupe, and briefly stopped in Puerto Rico. On his third, he
visited Trinidad, Grenada, Tobago, and Margarita, and he spotted

the mainland of South America—what is now Venezuela—but thinking it was just another island, he never landed there. His fourth and final voyage took him to Central America and the Panama islands.

Did Columbus ever figure out that he hadn't gotten to Asia?

With each trip Columbus kept trying to push westward, believing if he could just get through these islands, he'd reach the ports of Japan and the Imperial Palace in China, the places he'd set out to find in the first place. Of course, he never did, but he died believing that all of the spots he'd visited in the Americas were actually parts of Asia.

Did Columbus have any other ships besides the three he took to the New World?

Yes. In all, Columbus captained the *Pinta*, the *Niña*, the *Santa Maria*, the *Gallega*, the *Maríagalante*, the *Cardera*, the *San Juan*, the *Capitana*, and the *Santiago de Palos*.

Did Christopher Columbus have any children?

He had two sons, Diego and Ferdinand, the eldest of whom (Diego) sailed with him on his fourth voyage to the New World when he was just 13 years old. Presumably, Ferdinand ended up with a gift bearing the inscription: "My Dad discovered the New World and all I got was this lousy T-shirt."

KINGS & QUEENS

The kings and queens of Europe have always been good for a diversion—scandals, beheadings, treachery, inquisitions. Looking at the colorful foibles of the past, you have to admit that our present-day leaders are pretty gray in comparison. Perhaps, solely for entertainment value, it's time to admit we made a mistake with this democracy fad and bring back the monarchy.

MARRY IN HASTE, EXECUTE IN LEISURE

Did any of Henry VIII's wives survive being married to him?

Oh, be fair: It's not like he executed *all* of them. Let's go through the roster. Catherine of Aragon: marriage annulled, died a natural death shortly thereafter; Anne Boleyn: beheaded; Jane Seymour: died in childbirth; Anne of Cleves: marriage annulled; Catherine Howard: beheaded; Catherine Parr: still alive and married to Henry when he died.

How long was Lady Jane Grey queen before she was beheaded?

A whopping nine days. Blame John Dudley, the lord chamberlain to King Edward VI, for getting her into such a mess. Dudley was an ambitious man. He had Edward's complete trust and was fortunate enough that the king was in the process of dying. Edward was a Protestant, and Dudley quickly devised a scheme to maintain his power with the royal family before Edward's Catholic sister Mary could come to the throne. His 17-year-old daughter-in-law, Lady Jane Grey, was the great-granddaughter of Henry VII, which he figured was a good enough lineage to make her the perfect vehicle for his plan. Dudley convinced the dying Edward to sign documents that skipped royal succession over both of his half sisters, Mary and Elizabeth, making Lady Jane queen of England upon his death and saving England from the scourge of Catholicism. It worked—for about a week and a half, anyway—until Mary challenged the succession and was quickly recognized as the legitimate ruler. Lady Jane had never wanted to be queen in the first place, but she and her husband were thrown into the Tower of London and beheaded within the year.

TWO FANATICAL CATHOLIC QUEENS NAMED MARY

Why was Bloody Mary called that?

We can assure you that it wasn't because she invented the tomato-based cocktail. Bloody Mary—Mary Tudor—was one of Henry VIII's daughters. She occupied the throne of England as Mary I after her half brother King Edward VI, but before her half sister, Queen Elizabeth I. Mary I earned her nickname not long after she came into reign. Her father had severed ties with the Roman Catholic Church, a move which Edward supported and continued under his crown. Mary, however, rescinded all of her brother's proclamations when she came into power and made it her crusade to bring Catholicism back to England. She began enforcing laws of heresy that resulted in the burning of more than 300 Protestants during the five years she held the crown. She became known as Bloody Mary, not to be confused with another fanatical Catholic of her era, Mary Queen of Scots.

Which queen's head got dropped and bounced across the floor after she was beheaded?

You're thinking of Mary, Queen of Scots. But it wasn't like anybody did it on *purpose*.

The executioner was a little nervous that day. He wasn't used to executing women, and now here were all these important people watching him do his job. And frankly, he screwed up. The first blow missed Mary's neck completely, cutting into the back of her skull. The second and third tries hit the neck but didn't sever it. Finally, the executioner took his ax and made a sort of grinding motion on the remaining sinew of her neck to finish the job.

You can imagine the sweat dripping down his brow. Luckily, though, there was still a chance to wow the onlookers with his crowd-pleasing showstopper of holding the severed head up triumphantly for all to see. He reached down and grabbed the queen's head firmly by her hair. . . .

As we said, he was more used to executing men. It hadn't occurred to him that Mary might be wearing a wig. As he stood up, the queen's head— her real hair gray and cut short— slipped out of the wig and fell to the floor. Imagine the poor guy's embarrassment.

Ask! Where can I see the death mask of Mary, Queen of Scots?

WHAT'S IN A NICKNAME?

How did "Ethelred the Unready" get his nickname?

Ethelred II, a little-known king of England, reigned from 978 to 1013 and again from 1014 to 1016. He had ascended the throne under suspicion after his half brother, King Edward the Martyr, was mysteriously assassinated. The difference in nicknames says it all: The murder of the beloved king created a cloud of distrust and disloyalty around Ethelred's rule. The distrust was so pervasive that he and his shadowy council of advisors were unable to organize a unified defense when the Danes invaded and took control over parts of England. Warfare calmed down as the Danes got busy setting up their own villages on the edges of England. Ethelred decided that this was an intolerable situation and sent armies to massacre the Danish settlers. The Danish king Sweyn I (known as "Forkbeard") reacted badly to this and invaded London. Ethelred fled to Normandy. When Sweyn died the next year, Ethelred's council of advisors convinced him to return and claim the crown. This provoked Sweyn's son Canute to ravage England all over again.

So, you can see why "the Unready" was a fitting nickname, except we'd be wrong to leave it at that. It turns out that his nickname in the 11th century was really Ethelred *Unraed,* which at the time meant "Ethelred the Badly Counseled."

Some royal nicknames were kind of insulting. Were the kings really called these things to their faces?

We suspect that some nicknames could've been used without offense (for example, Richard the Lion-Hearted, Vladimir the Saint, Charles the Wise, or Henry the Lion). However, we suspect that the really insulting nicknames could've gotten you killed—do you think Ivan would've *liked* being called "the Terrible"? People used them behind the king's back or, more often, when he was safely dead.

Here are some of our favorite nicknames that have been permanently affixed in the history books: Louis the Fat (Louis VI, France, 1108–1137), Louis the Quarrelsome (Louis X, France, 1314–1316), Pippin the Short (Pepin, England, 741–768), Charles the Bald (Charles II, France, 840–877), Charles the Fat (Charles II, France, 884–887), Charles the Simple (Charles III, France, 898–922), Henry the Fowler (Henry I, France, 919–936), Louis the Indolent (Louis V, France, 986–987), Philip the Amorous (Philip I,

France, 1060–1108), and a schizophrenic pairing: Charles the Mad and Charles the Well-Beloved, both referring to Charles VI (France, 1380–1422).

Finally, here's a mysterious one: John the Posthumous (John I, France, 1316). He was named that because he was born after the death of his father (Louis the Quarrelsome) and was proclaimed king as soon as he emerged from the womb. The infant king ruled for five days before he himself died—murdered, some say, by his crown-seeking uncle, Phillip the Tall (Phillip V, France, 1316–1322).

CHECKMATE!

What was the War of the Roses about?

It was a power struggle for the throne of England that occurred in 1422 when Henry VI was king. He was from the House of Lancaster, and the nobles of another family, the House of York, decided that he was weak enough to be overthrown. Here's where the roses come in: York's emblem was a white rose, and Lancaster's a red one. Edward IV of York won the throne from Henry VI after six years of war, but Henry won it back nine years later. In 1471, Edward again defeated Henry, and Henry died in the Tower of London.

Who was the British king who had his two young nephews killed so they couldn't take the throne?

When Edward (see above) died in 1483, his two sons were still children. Because he stole the crown fair and square, he assumed that one of them would become king. However, his brother, Richard of York, had other plans. He imprisoned the boys in the Tower of London and declared himself King Richard III. The boys were never seen again.

HEIRS IN THE SOUP

Was Queen Victoria from the House of Windsor?

No, she was from the House of Hanover. Lovingly devoted to her German husband Prince Albert, she changed her name to that of the German royal family: Saxe-Coburg-Gotha.

If Queen Elizabeth II was a direct descendent of Queen Victoria's, why isn't she also a Saxe-Coburg-Gotha?

Funny thing, that. During World War I, when England was losing a generation of young men fighting Germany, the family decided that a German name might be worth losing. Casting about for something suitable, they decided on "House of Windsor," naming themselves after one of their royal castles.

Who was the Windsor who built Windsor Castle?

Windsor was actually the place, not the builder, and the town had been a place of kings since the Saxon days of old. When that pesky Norman, William the Conqueror, took over England 900 years ago, he built what is now known as the Castle at Windsor. The location, then as now, overlooked the River Thames and seemed an ideal spot for acting like a sovereign big shot. Over the years, the British monarchs have agreed and continue to call it one of their many homes.

Why did Elizabeth decide to go by the hyphenated family surname Windsor-Mountbaden?

It was in tribute to her new husband, Phillip Mountbaden. She also decreed that all of her future descendents would take the name as well, except for princes and princesses, who would keep the Windsor name.

HOW TO SUCCEED WITHOUT REALLY TRYING

How old was Queen Elizabeth when she assumed the throne?

Which one? Never mind, it doesn't really matter because both Queen Elizabeth I and II were 25 when they were coronated.

Is Prince Charles related to all of the British kings and queens through history?

All but two: Charles II and James II.

Has Queen Elizabeth had the British throne the longest?

Not yet. Victoria held it the longest, for over 63 years. Queen Elizabeth II wouldn't hit that point until 2015. In that year, she'll be 89 years old.

NOW PLAYING AT THE PALACE

Which French King Louis built the Versailles palace?

The Sun King, Louis XIV. He ruled for 72 years. He was also notable for expelling all Protestants from France. Perhaps he was tired of them ringing his doorbell early on Sunday mornings.

Why was Louis XIV called "the Sun King"?

Louis XIV chose the sun as an emblem of his rule. He had it incorporated into decorations around the palace, within portraits and emblems, such as royal stamps, his crown, and scepter. He also had a picture of a sun traced into the palace gardens. Why the sun? It was the symbol of the Greek god Apollo, god of the arts and peace. The sun represented to Louis XIV all of the things he worked toward bringing to France during his rule: consistency and life.

Which French King Louis was reinstated to the throne after Napoleon was deposed from leadership?

Louis XVIII. What an ending to the French Revolution: After going to the trouble of killing the ruling class, the people ended up with a dictator, Napoleon. When he was exiled the first time, they got another king; then Napoleon came back for a few months and they got a dictator again. Finally, they got the same king back again. It's enough to make even the most idealistic rabble become discouraged and cynical. No wonder it got harder and harder to get a good mob going after that.

DIRT ON THE ROYALS

Is it true that Louis XIV never bathed?

That's slander and a damnable lie. Historians tell us he bathed once a year, whether he needed it or not.

RELATIVELY SPEAKING

Which recent English monarch married his or her first cousin?

"Recent" is relative, no pun intended. The noted Victorian queen, Queen Victoria, married her first cousin. For years she had refused to consider marriage. It was rumored she had a serious crush on the first prime minister, a Whig named Lord Melbourne, during these reluctant years. In 1840, she gave into parental pressure and married her cousin Prince Albert of Germany. Her reluctance disappeared more quickly than you can say, "Do you have Prince Albert in a can?" This was the 21-year-old Victoria's diary entry describing her honeymoon:

> I never, never *spent such an evening! My dearest, dearest dear Albert sat on a footstool by my side, and his excessive love and affection gave me feelings of heavenly love and happiness I never could have hoped to have felt before! He clasped me in his arms, and we kissed each other again and again! His beauty, his sweetness and gentleness—really, how can I ever be thankful enough to have such a* Husband! . . . *To be called by names of tenderness I have never yet heard used to me before was bliss beyond belief!*

They had an unusually happy marriage that produced nine children. When Albert died in 1861 at 42 years of age, Victoria was completely bereft. Many historians say she never fully recovered from her loss, and as a result, she chose never to marry again.

RIDE 'EM COWGIRL!

How could Catherine the Great have had sex with a horse?

Rumor had it that it was accomplished with a special harness—the horse was lowered onto her from above—and that she died when the harness broke and the horse crushed her. It's one of the naughtier sex stories in history, and it's completely, entirely untrue.

Catherine the Great was the German-born Queen of Russia, and she lived up to her nickname. During her 34-year reign (1762–96), she managed to expand Russia's borders, end uprisings in her kingdom, and advance the arts and sciences. What she didn't have was a good marital relationship. She was fortunate that the union brought her the crown in the end, but she was unfortunate in that when she wedded Czar Peter III, she married an impotent, feebleminded man.

Before becoming czar, Peter had joined a wacko cult called the Skoptzies, in which the members amputated their genitals for salvation. Fortunately, Peter didn't go that far, but regardless, he wasn't much interested in or capable of having sex. Catherine soon realized she would need to take lovers if she wanted intimacy. When she was young and beautiful, no one minded her infidelity much because Peter was incompetent and not well liked by either the Russian people or those who knew him personally. Most people were aware that her son, Paul, heir to the Russian throne, probably certainly wasn't Peter's child. But all of these things weren't what sparked the rumors. What started the horse rumors—and others equally appalling and imaginative—was that Catherine never *stopped* the practice of taking lovers, even as she grew older and older, still bedding young men while in her 60s. Visiting foreign dignitaries found this distasteful, despite the fact that male monarchs were far more profligate in their sexual relationships and practices.

What does "czar" mean in Russian?

Both *czar* (Russia) and *kaiser* (Germany) were derived from the name of Julius Caesar, leader of ancient Rome.

ADVANCE ON ROYALTIES

What are the differences between a duke, lord, sir, earl, baron, baronet, and prince?

The various distinctions were drawn long ago, but still hold true today. Here they are in order from top to bottom:

- Prince
- Duke
- Marquess
- Earl
- Viscount
- Baron is the lowest rank of the upper classes, having earned this title by faithful duty to the king or feudal lord, usually in the form of military service.
- A baronet is the highest-ranking class that can be bestowed upon a mere commoner like you or me. This title is also usually earned through faithful service to rulers.
- A lord, generally, is any of the above who get a title and property by hereditary right or by being born into the right family. "Sir" is simply the title used when addressing a knight or a baronet.

Often, some hereditary titleholders will hold other titles as well. For instance, the eldest son of the king or queen of England, aside from being a prince, is also automatically the Duke of Cornwall, no questions asked.

GOOD HAIR AND MANORS

What is it that made a house a manor?

The same thing that once made young American men go west: No, not gold—land.

A manor was an estate. It usually held a main, large house or small castle, a church, an apothecary, granaries, stables, etc. It also had enough land for cultivation and for one's serfs and indentured servants to have small houses and their own private plots of land as well. In a sense, a large manor was like a very small working village.

What did they call those really tall wigs worn in the royal courts by 18th-century men and women?

Perukes. Incidentally, the wigs and the behavior of the elite that wore them were the inspiration for the term "bigwig."

I FOUGHT THE LAW (& THE LAW WON)

No wonder bad boys and girls are so appealing. To those of us who spend our lives feeling fenced-in and controlled, outlaws offer vicarious thrills without personal risk. Better, of course, is to find the desperado impulse buried deep within our souls, to make a break for it, out of the beige cubicles and neat white picket fences that we think hold us captive. . . .

SMILE WHEN YOU SAY THAT, PARTNER

What was John Wesley Hardin's job before he became a gunfighter?

Before he reformed and took up honest work as a gunfighter, he was a lawyer.

Why did they call him "Billy the Kid"?

Partly it was because he was 17 when he committed his first murder and was dead before he was 22. Mostly, though, it was because he looked a lot like a goat. Regardless, calling him "the Kid" in front of his goatish face would've been a mistake because Henry McCarty (also known as William Bonney) hated the name and was a hot-tempered sort of guy. Billy killed six people in his four-year career (although he has been credited with many more in folklore).

Did Jesse James have a nickname?

Yes. His friends called him Dingus.

Was Bat Masterson's first name really Bat?

No, it was Bartholomew Masterson. He later called himself William Barclay. How he got the nickname *Bat* is still open to debate. One story is that it's because of the cane he carried, which he used as a weapon whenever possible before going for a gun. This philosophy was the result of a barroom gun battle in which he accidentally killed a woman friend in the crossfire. Other theories are that it's short for "Battling Bill Masterson," or an abbreviated version of his middle name. Regardless, there's an irony in that "Bat" better suited his later years when he traded his gun for a Remington typewriter. He'd moved to New York City and become a sports writer for the *Morning Telegraph*. In 1921, after two decades of being football Bat, basketball Bat, and baseball Bat, Masterson died with his boots on at his desk, typing out a story.

WILL FLOSSING PREVENT GUN DISEASE, DOCTOR?

Was Doc Holliday a real doctor?

When Wyatt Earp's gun-slinging pal wasn't drillin' people in other ways, he worked as a dentist.

CANNED AND ABLE

Who were the bank robbers who wore suits of armor?

That would be the Kelly Gang—four "bushrangers" (outlaws) led by Ned and Dan Kelly, who robbed banks in Australia in 1879 and 1880. Their most interesting contribution to the art of bankrobbing was their suits of armor, fashioned out of plow blades they'd stolen from farmers.

Three of the gang were caught by police in a hotel siege and killed. As the battle raged, Ned Kelly donned his armor and rushed the police line, trying to rescue his gang. Unfortunately, while the armor worked pretty well in protecting them from mortal wounds, it left their arms and legs exposed. Kelly's unarmored legs were his Achilles' heel. After being shot several times, the Aussie lost his ability to waltz with Matilda and was captured. Later that year, he was tried, convicted, and hung.

MEN IN TIGHTS

Did Robin Hood really exist?

No one knows for sure, but there isn't much evidence that he did. All we know is that he *should've* existed. Whether fact or fiction, the first mention of him was in medieval ballads. A popular song about a man named Robyn Hod swept England in those days. The first mention of him in writing doesn't appear until 1378, or thereabouts. William Langland's "Piers Plowman" contains a priest character who's so drunk he can't recite the Lord's Prayer, but the "rhymes of Robin Hood" flow freely from his lips. Over the years, the oral traditions of Robin Hood were put into writing and passed on as literature. With each retelling, the story was changed a little to fit the audience, and we've ended up today with the "robbing the rich to give to the poor" rendition that we know and love.

Ask! Where can I see a list of Robin Hood movies?

THAT'S DR. RIPPER TO YOU

Who was Jack the Ripper?

Nobody knows, but there are plenty of theories. In London, from August 31 to November 9, 1888, five prostitutes were killed and mutilated. Based on the precision with which "Jack" practiced his murders, some people believed that Jack the Ripper was a surgeon. One suspect was the royal physician, Sir William Gull. Another was Dr. Francis Tumblety, a reputed misogynist gynecologist whose personal effects included a collection of preserved uteruses. Tumblety was charged on suspicion for the murders of the four Whitechapel prostitutes in London, but fled to the U.S. In New York the police kept him under survellaince for some time but could not extradite him for the crime of suspicion. He died in St. Louis, a wealthy man, in 1903.

Still another Jack the Ripper suspect was Dr. Thomas Neill Cream. He was convicted for murdering five London prostitutes (not the ones associated with Jack the Ripper) with strychnine and hanged for his crimes. On the scaffolding he blurted out "I am Jack the–" just before the scaffolding bolt was drawn.

The London police received hundreds of letters from people claiming to be Jack. Only one was believed to be authentic. Part of a victim's kidney was enclosed, and the package's return address was "From Hell."

STRANGLERS IN THE NIGHT

Why are thugs called "thugs"?

In honor of the Thugs, a centuries-old criminal society in India. Its members robbed and murdered in honor of Kali, the Hindu goddess of destruction, who was the wife of Shiva. The Thugs always murdered by strangling because spilling blood was against their religion.

According to the *World Book Encyclopedia,* "In 1831, the British began a drive to end the practice, and it is now almost wiped out." Yikes–what do they mean by "almost"?

Is it true that the word "assassin" comes from "hashish"?

The word comes from *hashshashin* (hemp-eaters), a name given to a secretive band of Muslims in Persia and Asia Minor in the 11th through the 13th centuries. The shadowy group, officially called the Nizari Isma'ilites, supposedly smoked hashish and killed their enemies while under its influence. Led by Hasan-e Sabbah, who believed that terrorism was a sacred religious duty, the Nizari Isma'ilites created a secret network of propagandists, double agents, spies, and killers. Sabbah placed agents in enemy camps who then would patiently work their way into positions of trust, until the signal came to kill and slip into the night. They claimed many victims among generals and statesmen, including two caliphs. Although their murders and treachery have been well documented, historians believe that the story about getting high before assassinations may have been a myth of the time. Makes sense; hashish seems like the entirely wrong drug for a job that requires trickery, quick-wittedness, and fast footwork.

NOT-SO-WISE GUYS

How old is the Mafia?

Although everyone agrees that the Mafia started as a shadow organization in Sicily, what's amazing is that historians can't seem to agree on what the name means, or even whether it started in the ninth century, the 18th century, or somewhere in between.

Who were the first gangsters?

Less-evolved people have been acting like thugs for most of human history. However, the word "gangster" wasn't coined until 1896. The word first appeared in a newspaper in Columbus, Ohio, in April of that year. "Mobster" didn't appear until 1917, although the word "mob" first showed up in the 17th century, from *mobile vulgus* (Latin for "the fickle crowd").

Is the Mafia the world's biggest criminal organization?

Not even close. The Mafia has a few thousand active members worldwide; the ancient, even more mysterious Six Great Triads of China has close to 100,000.

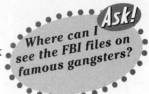

Where can I see the FBI files on famous gangsters?

A LAW UNTO HIMSELF

What did the J. stand for in J. Edgar Hoover?

John. Johnny Hoover!—now that would've been a great tough-guy, G-man sort of name. Why he chose to go by his middle name instead is anybody's guess.

> **What did the "G" in "G-men" stand for?**
> Government.

GOYS & DOLLS

Bugsy Siegal doesn't sound like an Italian name. How'd he get into the Mafia?

Benjamin "Bugsy" Siegal (he hated his nickname, by the way) was a young Jewish punk when "Lucky" Luciano discovered him. While Siegal wasn't from any particular crime family originally, Luciano was an equal-opportunity sort of guy. Together with Luciano and another Jewish kid named Meyer Lansky, Siegal formed one of the most powerful crime syndicates of all time.

They created Las Vegas as we know it, with Siegal at the lead. His Flamingo Hotel is still there in all of its dubious splendor. Siegel, however, isn't—he was rubbed out in 1947 when his associates discovered that he was not being totally honest with the money. Imagine that, a mobster not being trustworthy. What *is* this world coming to?

MAMA'S BOYS

Why did Ma Barker get her boys involved in a gang?

Kate "Ma" Barker, despite a popular myth that emerged after her death, wasn't really the brains behind the crimes of the Barker boys. Her biggest crime was harboring, excusing, and overindulging her criminal children—Freddy, Herman, Lloyd, and Doc—and their delinquent friends. Elmer H. Inman, a glasses-wearing, professor type, was the real mastermind. Others were Glen Leroy Wright and Raymond Karpavioz, also known as Alvin Karpis, which is why the gang was sometimes referred to as the Barker-Karpis Gang. In 1935, Ma Barker and son Freddy ended up catching some bullets from the FBI at their Florida hideout on Lake Weir. Both died.

THE GANG'S ALL HERE

Who ordered the Valentine Day's Massacre?

Al Capone.

What did Al Capone claim was his real business?

His business card identified him as a secondhand furniture dealer.

Were any of Al Capone's brothers also gangsters?

No. In fact, his brother Vince was a policeman in Omaha.

Where did "Scarface" Al Capone get his scar?

You're probably hoping for something ironic, like being scratched while saving a kitten from a tree? No such luck—he got knifed by a hood in a bar fight over some dame. It was 1917, he was 18 years old, and the punk was already on the road to ruin.

How did Al Capone die? In a hail of bullets?

Despite all the bootlegging, whoring, shakedowns, and murders, the law couldn't get Capone on anything more serious than income tax evasion. So they arrested him for that. He considered this a serious injustice, complaining that it was unconstitutional self-incrimination to make him report income from illegal activities. He sort of had a point but was sentenced to eleven years in jail anyway. He served eight years of his sentence, then retired to his luxurious estate in Florida in 1939. Eight years later, he died from an old case of syphilis.

Why did gangsters call a hundred dollar bill a "C-note"? Did those guys speak Latin?

It's true that the Latin word *centum* means hundred (which is why "C" was used in Roman numerals to mean a hundred). It's also the reason why American dollar bills once had a C on them. That's the reason gangsters called them C-notes, not because a bunch of wise guys were out late one night conjugating verbs in an after-hours Latin bar.

PUBLIC ENEMY NO. I

How did John Dillinger die?

Dillinger was not a nice guy, and he was the first criminal ever to be designated "Public Enemy Number 1" by the FBI. In one year, he had yielded about half a million dollars from daring bank heists. (Half a million in 1934 would be more than $3 million now.) He was brazen, even once robbing a police station when he needed new weapons. "A guy in this racket is living on borrowed time," he was quoted as saying. "Mine, something tells me, is short. When I go, I hope it's quick, in the midst of a thrill."

In spring of 1934, Dillinger got a face-lift, a dye job, grew a mustache, and had his fingerprints burned off with acid. He got cocky, thinking his disguise was enough. Despite a nationwide manhunt, he lived openly in Chicago with a waitress named Polly Hamilton, telling her his name was Jimmie Lawrence. Her landlady, Anna Sage, however, caught on to who he really was. Anna ran a whorehouse and was facing deportation to her native Romania, so she thought a good deed might get her a break from the authorities. She called the police and ratted on him.

Based on her information, sixteen federal agents staked out the Biograph Theatre in Chicago on a hot July night. After the movie, the agents moved in to arrest him. Seeing what was up, Dillinger ran toward an alley and drew his .38. He was immediately struck by three bullets and was dead in a few minutes. Two women were hit in the legs by stray bullets, but neither of them was Sage or Hamilton, who had made themselves scarce.

What movie did John Dillinger see the night he was ambushed by the G-men?

At least he saw a good movie before he died: *Manhattan Melodrama,* starring Clark Gable, William Powell, Myrna Loy, and Mickey Rooney. It's about two boyhood pals, one of whom becomes a gangster, and the other a policeman. The movie's still good fun. We give it $3\frac{1}{2}$ stars—just be careful who you watch it with.

Who was the "Lady in Red"?

Immediately after Dillinger's death, rumors quickly spread about a mysterious "Lady in Red" who had betrayed Dillinger by pulling out a handkerchief as she left the theater. Ironically, the lady dressed in red wasn't Anna Sage (Dillinger's real betrayer), but his unsuspecting date, Polly Hamilton, who was wearing a dark orange dress. Another irony: Turning Dillinger in didn't do Sage any good; she was deported anyway.

My grandmother has a stained handkerchief she says has gangster John Dillinger's blood on it. Is this possible?

Gruesome, yes, and also possible. We do know that ghoulish souvenir hunters dipped handkerchiefs and newspapers into the pool of Dillinger's blood on the sidewalk. It's possible that your grandmother was one of these ghouls, but we'd rather believe she's joking. Shine a light in her face and ask her: "Where was youse on the night of July 22, 1934?"

JUST LIKE ROMEO & JULIET, EXCEPT FOR THE GUNS

Did Bonnie and Clyde work with other bank robbers?

Not with any of the true professionals, who weren't too impressed with them. "They're giving bank robbery a bad name," complained John Dillinger. For one thing, Clyde was a little too quick on the trigger finger. The FBI blamed 13 murders on them during their two-year crime spree.

What gangster wrote a fan letter to Henry Ford about his cars?

That was Clyde Barrow. On April 10, 1934, he sat down and addressed a letter to Mr. Ford from a hideout where he and Bonnie Parker were holed-up in Florida. The letter, stamped "Received" by the Ford Motor Company three days later, read (mistakes and all):

> Dear Sir:
> While I still have got breath in my lungs I will tell you what a dandy car you make. I have drove Fords exclusively when I could get away with one. For sustained speed and freedom from trouble the Ford has got ever other car skinned and even if my business hasent been strictly legal it don't hurt enything to tell you what a fine car you got in the V-8.
> Yours truly,
> Clyde Champion Barrow

The next month, on May 23, 1934, both he and Bonnie died behind the wheel of a stolen, beige 1934 Ford V-8.

How many bullets hit Bonnie and Clyde when they were ambushed by lawmen?

One count puts it at 106.

YO HO, A PIRATE'S LIFE FOR ME

Were all pirates as bad as they've been portrayed in the Pirates of the Caribbean?

You mean the Disney ride? Not all of them. Some of them were worse, and they didn't sing so well, either.

Pirates gained a naughty reputation because, in essence, they were pretty naughty. Money was the overwhelming motivator in this line of work; one did what one had to do to obtain it.

Having said that, not all pirates were complete lawless rogues. Many ships were governed by a strict code of conduct, which all aboard were obligated to follow, oftentimes formulated by the crew themselves. For example, here's "The Articles on Board the *Revenge*," a ship under Captain John Phillips in the 18th century, drafted by the crew:

I. Every Man shall obey civil Command; the Captain shall have one full Share and a half in all Prizes; the Master, Carpenter, Boatswain and Gunner shall have one Share and quarter.

II. If any Man shall offer to run away, or keep any Secret from the Company, he shall be marroon'd, with one Bottle of Powder, one Bottle of Water, one small Arm, and Shot.

III. If any Man shall steal any Thing in the Company, or game, to the Value of a Piece of Eight, he shall be marroon'd or shot.

IV. If at any Time we should meet another Marroner that Man that shall sign his Articles without the Consent of our Company, shall suffer such Punishment as the Captain and Company shall think fit.

V. That Man that shall strike another whilst these Articles are in force, shall receive Moses's Law (that is, 40 Stripes lacking one) on the bare Back.

VI. That Man that shall snap his Arms, or smoak Tobacco in the Hold, without a Cap to his Pipe, or carry a Candle lighted without a Lanthorn, shall suffer the same Punishment as in the former Article.

VII. That Man that shall not kep his Arms clean, fit for an Engagement, or neglect his Business, shall be cut off from his Share, and suffer such other Punishment as the Captain and the Company shall think fit.

VIII. If any Man shall lose a Joint in time of an Engagement, shall have 400 Pieces of Eight; if a Limb, 800.

IX. If at any time you meet with a prudent Woman, that Man that offers to meddle with her, without her Consent, shall suffer present Death.

Where was "the Pirate Republic"?

It was Tortuga, in what is now known as the Cayman Islands. It started out as a stopover for buying preserved meat, but eventually the meat curers decided that looting and pillaging was more profitable than making beef jerky.

France had set up a little colony in Jamaica and had begun curing beef from cows that had been left behind when an earlier Spanish settlement was abandoned. Passing ships would anchor nearby, and the meat merchants would row out to sell their wares. However, the meat curers realized that they'd get more business if they were closer to a major shipping route, and so moved their business to Tortuga. (Tortuga means "turtle" in Spanish. Christopher Columbus had named the entire chain of islands *Las Tortugas* because the place was crawling with sea turtles. It still is.)

As with any harbor town at the time, Tortuga began accumulating sailors who had abandoned their ships. A number of them got themselves hired into the meat-curing business. Some of the rougher ones realized that they had a splendid opportunity that went beyond mere salt pork. After all, ship crews trusted them to approach in their canoes and board their ships bearing beef carcasses and sharp knives. Perhaps they could find a better use for those knives. . . .

After taking a number of Spanish ships by surprise, the jerky boys soon had enough ships and weapons to literally start a small navy and so launched their own pirating business. A regular den of thieves it became. The meat shops closed, and this little haven of turtles and bad guys became known as the Pirate Republic.

Ask! Any clues on where to find pirate treasure?

CRIME PAYS, AND IN SOME CASES IS AN ACT OF PATRIOTISM

What's the difference between a pirate and a buccaneer?

Not much in theory. There was once a distinction, a much clearer one than we draw these days. There were three types of men we commonly call pirates: privateers, buccaneers, and genuine pirates. Pirates were first on the scene toward the end of the 14th century. They were usually ex-sailors, and they were certainly true outlaws. The word pirate comes from the Latin *peirates,* meaning "attacker." Other English words for these roving bands of seafarers were *rogues, rovers,* and from the Spanish: *picaroons.* They often couldn't find work anywhere else, so they hopped aboard with other disreputables and set off to steal their income.

Buccaneers were British, French, and Dutch settlers in the Caribbean who, as mentioned above, had begun as meat merchants before turning to piracy. The name came from the French word *boucanier,* meaning literally "he who cures meat." Although this group liked to call themselves "the Brethren of the Coast," others called them other names (some unprintable): The Dutch referred to them as *zeerovers,* where we got the word "sea-rovers"; the French: *flibustiers.* (This last one eventually got transformed by English politicians into "filibuster," that is, someone who hijacks a legislative floor. But that's another story.)

Privateers were quite different in one very large respect: They were legal and considered a legitimate form of economic war. They used privately owned fleets to ransack the cargo-laden ships of the enemy. The fleets were provided by wealthy merchant-investors who received a cut of the loot. Privateers often operated under outright immunity from government officials (or at the very least, a wink and a nod), as long as they agreed to ransack only enemy ships.

HANG YOUR HEAD, EDWARD TEACH

Was Blackbeard a pirate or a privateer?

The infamous Blackbeard (Edward Teach) was a sort of hybrid, a cross between a pirate and a privateer. He was ruthless and illegally terrorized ships of all nations off the eastern coast of the United States, but he had a deal with the colonial governor of North Carolina, Charles Eden. This meant that Eden offered Teach the protection of his ports in exchange for a portion of the wealth he seized from other ships. However, the partnership didn't help Blackbeard in the end—Teach was finally captured, shot, decapitated, and his head hung from the mast of his captor's ship.

Wasn't Sir Francis Drake a pirate at some point in his career?

All through his career, actually. He made his living by smuggling slaves and pirating Spanish ships. His entire "voyage around the world" was funded by Queen Elizabeth and was, in essence, a thinly-veiled privateering racket to plunder Spanish ships and settlements. It was only because the British hated the Spanish and that his expedition was so financially successful to the crown that he was knighted instead of hanged.

THE KIDDS ARE ALL RIGHT

Was Captain Kidd as bad a pirate as his legend says?

Captain William Kidd was a privateer, not a pirate. England's East India Company was one of his financial backers, and French ships were considered fair game. However, in the course of his tour, Kidd took a French ship that was sailed by Moors. To preserve ties with India, the East India Company railroaded him. Kidd was arrested in Boston and transported to England for trial. Kidd was not allowed to present his evidence; the jury found him guilty of piracy, and he was hanged.

Did Captain Kidd have any little Kidds?

He had two. Sara and Elizabeth Kidd lived with their mother, Sara Oort Kidd, on 56 Wall Street in New York City when William Kidd was put to death in 1701. While waiting to be hung, Kidd confessed no crimes to the chaplain, only that his greatest sorrow was dying without the chance to say good-bye to his wife and children back home.

Why did pirates make prisoners walk the plank when they could've just tossed them overboard?

You've got the instincts of a pirate all right. It turns out that they *did* toss them overboard, and they *didn't* really make them walk the plank. The walking-the-plank myth was first introduced in Robert Louis Stevenson's classic *Treasure Island* and has since been reinforced by pirate literature from *Peter Pan* to *Captain Blood*. (Stevenson was also the source for the most famous, yet completely fictitious, pirate song that goes "Sixteen men on a dead man's chest / Yo-ho-ho and a bottle of rum . . .")

Besides tossing victims overboard, typical punishments by real pirates included:

- ◆ **Flogging.** This treatment was universally popular at the time, on and off the high seas.

- ◆ **Man Overboard.** While this could be as simple as merely tossing the captive or prisoner overboard, it was sometimes varied to relieve the boredom of a long trip. Sometimes a man would be tied to one end of a rope and dragged until he died from drowning or exhaustion. Perhaps this was how waterskiing was invented.

◆**Dunking.** This was less popular, as it required dunking the prisoner then hoisting him back up again, suspending him for hours above the water. It was too time-consuming, and aside from the initial spluttering and choking, not that entertaining.

◆**Marooning.** This was the most common form of punishment for serious offenses like desertion. A sailor was either placed on a raft or left on a deserted island to die. If left in the water, he was often mercifully given a pistol to kill himself before the sharks got him.

SKULL AND BONES SOCIETY

Argh, matey! Where did the Jolly Roger flag come from?

The skull and crossbones image was used to represent death long before the era of pirates. It was seen a lot during plagues to warn that someone inside a house, ship, or room was afflicted.

Because the skull-and-crossbones had come to mean "danger, stay away," it seemed like a fitting accessory to be hoisted on a pirate ship. Why was it called the "Jolly Roger" when its meaning was anything but jolly, you might well ask? (Go ahead and ask. We'll wait for you.)

There are several theories that we've collected from some otherwise reliable factmongers. Here they are arranged in order of what we consider least likely to most likely:

◆The name came from the French *joli rouge,* meaning "pretty red." Supposedly, pirates were in the practice of dipping their flags in red paint or even blood. However, since the name refers to a black-and-white flag with no trace of red, this sounds like after-the-fact linguistic gymnastics. Admittedly, some pirate ships began displaying a *red* Jolly Roger to indicate that they were even more dangerous than ordinary pirates. However, the term "Jolly Roger" predates this practice.

◆ Asian pirates called themselves *Ali Rajas* or "Kings of the Sea," and subsequent British pirates butchered it to Jolly Roger. (Cute, but it also leaves us unconvinced.)

Ask!

Where can I see the words of some real pirate songs?

◆ Here's what we consider most likely: The term "Roger" had been in use in the English language since the middle ages, meaning "devil" or "rogue." Although today we define the word "jolly" as "happy" or "jovial," the term once meant "brave." (Thus, the song "For He's a Jolly Good Fellow" was meant to pay tribute to someone's bravery, not his cheerfulness.) We think "Jolly Roger" makes perfect sense as a name for a skeleton flying above a throng of brave rogues. That's our preferred story, and we're sticking to it.

PRESIDENTS & THEIR VICES

From Martin Van Buren and his concealed weapons to John Tyler nearly losing his marbles, there's something comforting in seeing human-ness in the leaders of our country. Therefore, it's under-standable that among all the questions received at "Ask Jeeves," some of the most frequent and the most popu-lar are about those who've been in the top, elected po-sitions in U.S. politics.

GREAT WHITE FATHERS

How many presidents didn't have kids?

A disproportionate number of presidents named James: James Madison, James Polk, and James Buchanan. George Washington had no children of his own, but raised Martha's children from her

PRESIDENTS & THEIR VICES 167

previous marriage. Her children certainly considered him a father, as is evidenced by the fact that they allowed him and Martha to raise their children (Martha's grandchildren) while he served as President.

How many U.S. presidents have been divorced?

Just one: Ronald Reagan.

Did any presidents have adopted kids?

Yes. Including Martha Washington's children that George adopted, there were two others: Andrew Jackson and Ronald Reagan.

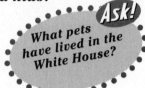

What pets have lived in the White House?

THE BODY IMPOLITIC

Wasn't JFK pretty sick during his presidency?

He was quite sick. During his childhood, back problems, jaundice, and other ailments kept Kennedy scrawny and weak. He suffered from two other serious problems: Addison's disease, in which the body can't produce sufficient amounts of the crucial immunity-boosting hormone cortisol, and a degeneration of the spine, probably due to repeat injuries. He also suffered the physical complications of having contracted malaria during World War II.

While serving in Congress, he underwent numerous steroid shots and back surgeries. There were at least four incidents prior to his death in 1963 where he had last rites administered by priests. During his presidency, though, Kennedy was healthier than he'd been in a while. Because so much of his appeal was based on his boyish good looks and athleticism, he went to great lengths to conceal his illnesses from the public.

Who was the first vice president to officially become acting president when the real president was incapable of performing his duties?

Believe it or not, George Bush. On July 13, 1985, while Reagan was having a tumor removed from his colon, he transferred presidential power to his vice president. Officially, the switch occurred at 11:28 A.M. Eight hours later, power was transferred back.

DEPARTMENT OF LABOR AND STATISTICS

How many of the first five U.S. presidents were born in England?

Zero. Of the first five—George Washington, John Adams, Thomas Jefferson, James Madison, and James Monroe—John Adams was the only one not born in the colony of Virginia. He was from the Massachusetts Bay colony.

Who was the first president born in a hospital?

Jimmy Carter. Until well into the 20th century, most people were born at home.

Which president was born Leslie King, Jr.?

Gerald Ford. His mother remarried and renamed him after her new husband.

My history teacher says that the Constitution says that presidents have to be native born but that eight presidents were not actually born in the United States. How can that be?

The first eight presidents were born in the American *colonies* before the Constitution was written—in fact, legally before the United States even existed.

AGE BEFORE BEAUTY

Some say John Kennedy, some say Teddy Roosevelt, so I'm confused: Who was the youngest American president?

Okay, pay attention, because this is confusing if you don't: Kennedy at 43 was the youngest person *elected* president, but he wasn't the youngest president. Roosevelt was vice president when McKinley was assassinated, elevating Teddy to the presidency when he was a mere 42.

EXIT THIS WAY

How many U.S. presidents have resigned from office?

One. Richard Nixon.

How many U.S. vice presidents have resigned from office?

Two: John Calhoun resigned in a policy dispute with the president, and Spiro Agnew resigned after it was discovered he'd been taking bribes.

Which vice president held office for the shortest amount of time?

Of the four vice presidents who've left office during the month of April in their first terms, Vice President Andrew Johnson held it the shortest at 40 days. But William Rufus Devane King is the only vice president to *die* within months of taking the office. He also holds the honor of being the only vice president to be sworn in on foreign soil (Havana, Cuba) and the only vice president to never even make it to Washington while in office. He has the second shortest vice presidential term on record, after Johnson.

SHOOTING FOR THE PRESIDENCY

What did John Wilkes Booth, Lincoln's killer, do for a living?

He was an actor.

Did Abraham Lincoln ever see his assassin perform on stage?

Yes. John Booth was not quite as celebrated as his brother Edwin, who was the most famous actor in the country at the time. Nor was he as respected as his father Junius, who had been the country's premiere Shakespearean actor. Still, John was very popular, especially with the ladies, and made as much as $30,000 a year (about $325,000 in modern dollars). Lincoln admired

Booth's melodramatic style very much and once invited him to visit the White House. Booth declined.

What state motto did John Wilkes Booth shout after he shot Abraham Lincoln?

A state motto? What are the choices? "I have found it!"; "The crossroads of America!"; "Famous potatoes!" We think not. Actually, it was Virginia's motto he shouted after jumping onto the stage: *"Sic semper tyrannis!"* ("Thus always to tyrants!").

My mom doesn't want me to become president because "it's too dangerous." What are the chances of being assassinated on the job?

Not that bad. Only four of the 43 so far have been killed by assassins, which is fewer than 10 percent. Tell your mom that it's about the same odds as working for the post office. (Okay, we're kidding about that last part. Please don't reroute our mail to Bulgaria again.)

Where was Lucretia Garfield when her husband and president, James Garfield, was shot?

She was recuperating from a nasty bout with malaria in their summer home. She survived; he did not.

Who took the live footage of the John F. Kennedy assassination?

A guy named Abraham Zapruder, owner of a Jennifer Juniors clothing store, recorded it on an amateur camera. His receptionist stood nearby in case his vertigo made him dizzy and he had to sit down. He just wanted a shot of the president and had no idea his bit of film was going to make history.

FAITH OF OUR FATHERS

Were any U.S. presidents not Christians?

If you judge them by the fruits of their actions, we suppose someone could make a case that a number of them were not, regardless of what faith they claimed. However, Abraham Lincoln was one who specifically rejected Christianity, even writing a pamphlet called *Infidelity,* which sought to disprove the Bible generally and the idea of Jesus being the son of God specifically. Later, as a politician, he succumbed to pressure to mention God in speeches but pointedly did not mention Jesus.

Thomas Jefferson attended an Episcopal church but refused to discuss his religious beliefs during his election campaign, and so was accused by rabble-rousing preachers of being ungodly and in league with Satan. Actually, he believed in the moral teachings of Jesus, but not in his divinity.

How old was George Washington when he chopped down the cherry tree?

Sorry to burst your bubble, but the cherry tree story's just a myth (where've you been, my friend?). It doesn't mean he wasn't ethical as a child, however. As a matter of fact, there's evidence George was extremely moral in his formative years. As a schoolboy, he wrote rules of behavior for himself into an exercise book that still survives today. What's not clear is whether it was his own idea or that of his mother or schoolteacher. Decide for yourself. Following are some of them (rendered in his own boyhood spelling, capitalization, and punctuation):

Turn not your Back to others especially in Speaking, Jog not the Table or Desk on which Another reads or writes, lean not upon any one.

Use no Reproachfull Language against any one neither Curse nor Revile.

Play not the Peacock, looking every where about you, to See if you be well Deck't, if your Shoes fit well, if your Skokings Sit neatly, and Cloths handsomely.

While you are talking, Point not with your Finger at him of Whom you Discourse nor Approach too near him to whom you talk especially to his face.

Be not Curious to Know the Affairs of Others neither approach those that Speak in Private.

It's unbecoming to Stoop much to ones Meat Keep your Fingers clean & when foul wipe them on a Corner of your Table Napkin.

YOUR OL' FURRY PAL GROVER

How much older was Grover Cleveland than his wife, Frances?

Twenty-eight years older: She was 21, and he was 49. Cleveland was the first and only president to marry in the White House. The public went crazy over the couple. They saw her as the young gal who put the reigns on an old codger, their bachelor president; they were most beloved. However, the story has a twist: The couple had had a different type of relationship prior to their romance. She was his ward. When her father, Cleveland's former law partner, Oscar Folsom, died in a carriage accident when Frances was 11, he left Cleveland his estate. Grover Cleveland spent the rest of Frances's childhood financially and emotionally supporting her and her mother.

What president was nicknamed "Big Steve"?

Grover Cleveland. He was a big man, weighing about 280 pounds, and his first name was Stephen (Grover was his middle name). He was also called "Uncle Jumbo," presumably not by his friends.

THREE LAWS OF REAL ESTATE

Besides Grant, is there anyone else buried in Grant's Tomb?

Yes. His wife, Julia Dent Grant.

Where can I see a picture of Grant's tomb? **Ask!**

Was Camp David named for the guy in the Bible who killed Goliath?

No. The presidential retreat was founded by Franklin Roosevelt, who named it Shangri-La. Dwight Eisenhower renamed it in honor of his grandson, David Eisenhower. That name stuck. David's only other claim to fame since was that he married Julie Nixon while her father was in the White House.

POPULARITY CONTEST

Who was the first presidential candidate to be endorsed by TV Guide?

Ronald Reagan. *TV Guide* can also be remembered as the first print venue to publish the conservative Republican coalition's "Contract With America," which helped Newt Gingrich capture the House in the 1996 campaign.

Which president received the most Electoral College votes?

Well, George Washington won 100% of the electoral votes when his name was put up for election.

Second-best was Richard Nixon in 1972, who got 520 electoral votes against George McGovern's 17. John Hospers of the Libertarian Party also won 1. This took place less than two years before Nixon was forced to resign from the office, mind you. Just goes to show you that your mother was right: Popularity is no substitute for character.

Who was the most unpopular president in history?

Probably John Tyler, who took over Harrison's presidency following his death. After Tyler vetoed key points of his own Whig Party's program, his entire cabinet resigned, except one member. An armed mob stormed the White House and threw rocks through its windows, and members of his party introduced an impeachment resolution in the House of Representatives. (It failed 127 to 83.) Still, spurned by both parties, Tyler retired after finishing his one partial term. Teddy Roosevelt summed him up 75 years later: "Tyler has been called a mediocre man, but this is unwarranted flattery. He was a politician of monumental littleness."

A BLOODY CAMPAIGN

What happened in the duel between Alexander Hamilton and Aaron Burr?

America's most infamous duel took place on July 11, 1804, in Weehawken, New Jersey. Burr and Hamilton had become political rivals when Burr won a Senate seat that had belonged to Hamilton's father-in-law. When Burr left the vice presidency and ran an unsuccessful campaign for New York governor, he was the victim of a vicious smear campaign that he thought Hamilton might've had a hand in. Afterward, when Hamilton made some negative statements about him in the press, Burr challenged him to a duel. Hamilton was killed, but Burr's "victory" made him a political and social pariah, and murder charges hung over his head in New York and New Jersey.

A few years later, Burr got himself into even further disgrace when he was caught putting together a private army with the hope of conquering parts of Louisiana and Mexico and creating his own kingdom. He was tried for treason, but escaped conviction on a technicality. After hiding out in Europe for a few years and piling up his debt, he had to quickly leave to escape debtors' prison. Returning to New York, Burr managed to get the old murder charges dropped and began practicing law again. Still, after personal setbacks, including the death of his beloved daughter and a disastrous late-in-life marriage and divorce, he lived a life "severed from the human race" (as he put it) and died forgotten in 1833 at the age of 80.

DON'T FORGET THE ADDRESS

How many is the "four score and seven years" mentioned in Lincoln's Gettysburg Address? What year was he referring to?

A "score" is equal to 20. Abraham Lincoln gave his speech in 1863. We'll let you do the math to find the famous year because if we just *gave* you the answer you wouldn't *learn* anything.

AND OTHER THINGS LINCOLN SAID

Where did the phrase "A house divided against itself cannot stand" come from?

Originally from the Bible: "Any kingdom divided against itself is laid waste; and any city or house divided against itself shall not stand" (Matthew 12:25). Abraham Lincoln popularized the verse in his speech accepting the Republican nomination for U.S. Senate from Illinois in June of 1858.

PRESIDENTIAL PERKS & QUIRKS

What U.S. president slept through most of his term?

President David Rice Atcheson. He was president for one day—March 4, 1849. James Polk's term ended then, but Zachary Taylor refused to be sworn in on a Sunday so the job went automatically to the senate president pro tem. "I slept most of that Sunday," Atcheson admitted, and Taylor was sworn in the next day.

Who was on his knees playing marbles when told he had become president?

John Tyler. William Henry Harrison had died a month into his term, and on April 6, 1841, Tyler was found deep in a game of aggies when given the news that he was the first vice president to succeed a dead president. Two decades later, Tyler apparently lost those marbles. He renounced his citizenship and joined the Confederacy.

Which U.S. president threw the most opening-day baseballs?

Franklin D. Roosevelt, as he was president for more opening-day baseball seasons than any other president.

Did any president not graduate from high school?

Three didn't even graduate from grade school: Andrew Jackson, Andrew Johnson, and Zachary Taylor.

Why didn't Teddy Roosevelt celebrate Valentine's Day?

Both his wife and mother died on Valentine's Day in 1884. He was so distraught that he retired from politics for two years.

DANGEROUS PRECEDENTS

When in American history was it a crime to criticize the president?

It was during the second half of John Adams's administration, which has become known as the Federalist Reign of Terror. Under the Alien and Sedition Acts, it became a crime to criticize the president or the government. It got so bad that his vice president, Thomas Jefferson, stopped signing his letters, correctly assuming that government agents were reading his mail. More than twenty newspaper editors and a member of the House of Representatives were jailed. (Representative Matthew Lyon got four months in jail and a $1,000 fine for writing an editorial in a Vermont newspaper; his constituents re-elected him while he was in jail and paid his fine.) The law finally expired after Jefferson became president.

Who was on Richard Nixon's "Enemies List"?

Literally hundreds of people and organizations. The list was given to government agencies, like the IRS, with quiet presidential orders to harass the people on it. He wanted payback.

Some of the more famous names on the list included movie

stars, politicians, and media folks, including Carol Channing, Jane Fonda, Dick Gregory, Judith Martin ("Miss Manners"), Steve McQueen, Joe Namath, Paul Newman, Gregory Peck, Edward Kennedy, Edmund Muskie, Harold Hughes, Walter Mondale, William Proxmire, Jack Anderson, Rowland Evans, Julian Goodman, Marvin Kalb, Joseph Kraft, Dan Rather, James Reston, and Daniel Schorr.

Nixon's list also targeted an odd assortment of groups like the National Education Association, the American Civil Liberties Union, the National Organization for Women, National Cleaning Contractors, Philip Morris, the Urban League, MIT (Massachusetts Institute of Technology), the World Bank, and Harvard Law School.

IT PROBABLY WASN'T LINDA LOVELACE

Who was "Deep Throat"?

We don't know yet. There are those who believe that Deep Throat didn't really exist—that Bob Woodward's crucial Watergate informant was a composite of several Washington insiders who knew the ins and outs of Richard Nixon's White House.

This is denied by Woodward. He is one of only four people who know his true identity: Woodward, Carl Bernstein, *Washington Post* editor Ben Bradlee, and Deep Throat himself (if "he" really is a he). None of them are talking, and Woodward says he won't reveal anything until after Deep Throat's death. (He has dropped some tantalizing clues in his writings, including that Deep Throat was a smoker who had a tendency to gossip and drink too much scotch.)

That doesn't mean that Washington insiders haven't had their own pet theories. White House lawyer John Dean thinks that it was Alexander Haig, Nixon's chief of staff. Many people think it was FBI associate director W. Mark Felt or Leonard Garment, White House counsel. Garment points the finger at political operative John Sears. Other names include CIA director Richard Helms, acting FBI director Pat Gray, both of whom had the knowledge and the motive of being at odds with

Nixon. Other suspects include Assistant Attorney General Henry Petersen, Deputy White House Counsel Fred Fielding, future CIA director William Casey, secretary of state Henry Kissinger, CIA officials Cord Meyer and William Colby, FBI officials Charles Bates and Robert Kunkel, and even present-day journalist Diane Sawyer, who worked in Nixon's press office at the time.

What did Vice President Martin Van Buren always have beside him when he presided over the Senate?

A pair of pistols.

NOT JUST ANOTHER PRETTY FAITH

Throughout history, people's faith in a religion has sometimes brought out their best, and oftentimes their worst. Who first formulated the Golden Rule? When can Amish drive cars? Let's take a flying leap of faith and see if any revelations come.

THE FARMER IN THE HELL

Where does the term "pagan" come from?

Like most English words, from Latin. The word comes from the root word *paganus*, which means "peasant." During the mass conversion of Rome to Christianity, the peasants and farmers were the last to be converted, and so the childish name-calling began.

A WEALTH OF ENLIGHTENMENT

Did most founders of major religions live in humble surroundings?

With the notable exception of one who was born in a manger, a disproportionate number had anything but humble beginnings. The founder of Buddhism, Siddhārtha, was a prince in what is now Nepal, who abandoned opulent wealth (not to mention a wife and baby) to wander as a holy man. Similarly, Lao-tze, the founder of Taoism, was said to have *also* been a prince who *also* lived in a nearby principality during exactly the same time. And Islam's Muhammad was raised by relatives in a nomadic desert tribe after his parents died. But in his 20s he married a rich widow, allowing him the luxury of pursuing his spiritual quests, unhindered by the burdens of want.

A SIMPLE CONCEPT, SO HARD TO LIVE

Who invented the Golden Rule?

Since the idea is so simple—"Do unto others as you would have them do unto you"—most religions and philosophies have some variation on it. However, the earliest known rendition came from Confucius (551–479 B.C.): "What you do not wish for yourself, do not do to others."

PHRASING A COIN

Isn't the United States a country with strict church/state separation? Why then do the coins say, "In God We Trust"?

The phrase first appeared on coins during the Civil War. The idea came from a letter that Treasury Secretary Salmon Chase got from an influential Pennsylvania minister named Reverend

M. R. Watkinson. "You are probably Christian," Watkinson wrote. "One fact touching our currency has hitherto been seriously overlooked. I mean the recognition of the Almighty God in some form on our coins." Watkinson advocated replacing the "goddess of liberty" with a more Christian-friendly design, adding that "no possible citizen could object. This would relieve us from the ignominy of heathenism. This would place us openly under the Divine protection we have personally claimed. From my heart I have felt our national shame in disowning God as not the least of our present national disasters."

Then, as now, politicians knew the danger of alienating religious folk. While Chase disregarded Watkinson's design suggestions, he took the idea of putting some sort of religious inscription on the coins. Chase requested that his staff come up with the shortest possible motto so it would fit onto the coins. Although "Yay, God!" would've been shorter, he finally settled on "In God We Trust," figuring it was short enough, dignified, more or less nondenominational, and it came from a verse of the *Star Spangled Banner* to boot ("and this be our motto / 'In God is Our Trust' "). Chase authorized adding the phrase to some of the existing coin designs.

Chase left office, and the designs of coins continued to change in the following years. With the war over, the slogan appeared on some coins and didn't on others, according to the whims of coin designers and politicians. In the early 1900s, Teddy Roosevelt tried to get the slogan banned. Finally, though, in 1954, during the height of McCarthyism, overenthusiastic anti-Communists passed a law mandating that the phrase *must* appear on America's money. At about the same time, the zealots also added the phrase "under God" to the Pledge of Allegiance. Both actions were designed to make it easy to differentiate the good, God-fearing Americans from those godless communists.

Has anybody tried to remove "In God We Trust" from America's coins?

Considering both the church/state and God/mammon issues, it's not surprising that some people have objected to the phrase. In 1996, the Freedom from Religion Foundation sued to have the slogan removed from United States money. A federal judge ruled against them, arguing somewhat illogically that " 'In God We Trust' is not a religious phrase."

In a country with so many people taking pride in their public displays of personal piety, you have to admire Theodore Roosevelt. He was the last president brave enough to try to get the slogan removed from coins. Although he was unsuccessful—and despite curses and fulmination from pulpits all over the country—his career wasn't struck dead by political lightning.

WADE IN THE WATER

When running from the Egyptians, how did the Israelites cross the Red Sea in a night? It's about 150 miles wide!

Good question. Here's what our biblical consultants say: "Red Sea" was apparently a translation error from the days when scholars were rendering the Bible into English for King James I. The original Hebrew called it a "sea of reeds," which historians say probably refers not to the Red Sea, but to a swamp of lakes and marshes.

THE TRUTH ABOUT CATS & GODS

Why did the Egyptians worship cats?

If you're an avid cat person, the answer of course is self-evident: Because cats are divine. Egyptians literally believed that to be true, to the point that if a household cat died, its owners would shave their eyebrows in mourning and lovingly transport the cat carcass to one of the cities devoted to mummifying cats for their journey to the next world. (They apparently didn't make it. In 1888, about 300,000 cat mummies were discovered still lounging around this world in the ancient city of Beni Hassan. We guess it illustrates once again how hard it is to get cats to go where you want them to.)

There were practical reasons for worshipping cats, though. The Egyptians were very dependent on grains for their main staples of bread and beer, and they knew how much the cats contributed to their lives and economy by keeping rats and mice in check.

Unfortunately, this worship of the cat had its downside, too. In 525 B.C., the Persians went to war with the Egyptians. Mindful of the Egyptians' religion, the Persians lined up a row of cats in front of their warriors. Egyptian soldiers were put into a crisis of faith—they quickly discovered that they couldn't swing a sword or fire an arrow for fear of hurting a cat and "hissing off" the cat goddess Pascht. The wily Persians quickly defeated the Egyptians. It was a cat-aclysm and a cat-astrophe.

Whatever happened to the 300,000 cat mummies they discovered in Beni Hassan?

They were dug up with tractors and sold for $18.43 a ton to an English fertilizer company.

Were any cats put to death for witchcraft during the Salem witch trials?

In America, no cats were harmed in the making of the Salem witch trials. Perhaps the Salem town elders learned a lesson from the witch hunts of Europe, in which hundreds of thousands of cats were killed for being in league with the devil. As a result, the devil got his due: Rats suddenly had free reign, and plagues ravaged the continent.

Although no cats were put to death, 20 people were, along with two of their dogs.

NEARER MY RA TO THEE

How many gods did the ancient Egyptians have?

More than 2,000. The greatest of these was the sun god, Ra. According to the Egyptians' creation story, the ocean was all that existed in the beginning. Then from the water came an egg (some versions say a flower). Ra emerged from it, eventually drying the lands—in Egypt's case, perhaps a little too well.

CLAIM TO INFAME

Did King Ferdinand and Queen Isabella do anything significant besides bankrolling Columbus's expedition?

Their other big act in 1492 was exiling all 200,000 Jews who lived in Spain under the threat of death. The expulsion of Jews was part of a much larger religious "cleansing" that the two had begun 12 years earlier, when they had likewise driven the Moslems out of Spain. As part of the effort, they instituted the Spanish Inquisition: imprisoning, torturing, and killing those suspected of insufficient zeal in following Roman Catholic teachings.

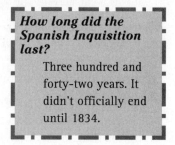

How long did the Spanish Inquisition last?

Three hundred and forty-two years. It didn't officially end until 1834.

WHO PUT THE "GRIM" IN PILGRIM?

When did the Pilgrims get that name?

Long after they'd all died and moved on to the next new world. For two centuries, the relatively obscure little colonists had been simply called "Founders" or "Forefathers." This changed in 1854 when a publisher got his hands on the journal of William Bradford. Bradford had been governor of the Plymouth Colony during its founding years two centuries earlier. Publishing his journal was a blockbuster event, which generated a great deal of hoopla and hype, and ultimately led to the United States adopting Thanksgiving as a national holiday. It also inadvertently gave a new name to the colonists. Within his journal, Bradford mentioned that the little band of religious separatists considered themselves "pilgrims" of a sort when they left Holland. People in the 19th century, trying to find a name to differentiate these forefathers from all the other forefathers of the nation, retroactively attached the name "Pilgrims" to the colonists.

Was there any difference between the Puritans and the Pilgrims?

The Puritans were the grim followers of Oliver Cromwell, who had gained control of England in 1649 after a bloody civil war. They got their name from their enemies who taunted them about wanting to "purify" both the Church of England and society. (They were also sometimes called "Roundheads" because they cut their hair short.) After their victory, the Puritans got a chance to remake their world, closing theaters and other places of amusement, banning the celebration of Christmas, and crushing those who got in their way. However, after nine years in power, Cromwell eventually died, and English royalty seized control of the government again, to almost everybody's relief.

Years before this, though, the Puritans had split into several factions. One of the biggest was a faction called the Separatists who had given up on reforming the Church of England and had begun their own independent congregations. One group of English Separatists were the people now better known as the "Pilgrims." Other Separatists moved to Rhode Island and founded the Baptist Church, while still others landed in Massachusetts Bay and founded the Congregationalists.

After Cromwell died, many of his Puritan followers decided it was best to get out of the country. They also ended up in Massachusetts, where they went to work expanding their influence and trying to pass laws to spoil the fun of settlers who had already moved there. For example, they successfully banned Christmas celebrations for a while in Boston and closed down some of the pubs and theaters. They also founded Harvard and Yale.

People nowadays confuse the Pilgrims with the Puritans. That's strange because, compared with the Puritans, the Pilgrims were hippies. Despite the image invented in the 19th century of grim people wearing dark clothes with buckles, Pilgrim men and women wore bright clothes of red, green, and violet (see page 119). They were fun-loving, democratic, good-natured, and frank about matters concerning love and sex—pretty much the antithesis of the severe, militantly authoritarian Puritans.

BELIEVE WHAT YOU WANT, AS LONG AS IT CONFORMS

Did the Puritans and Pilgrims believe in freedom of religion?

Sure, for themselves. However, neither had much tolerance toward other groups.

How long is America's tradition of freedom of religion?

Not that long. (Some would claim that it *still* hasn't arrived, but that might be overstating things a bit.) Although freedom of religion was guaranteed in the Bill of Rights, court rulings held that it applied only to the *federal* government, leaving state governments free to be as discriminatory as they wanted to be. Until the mid-1800s, a number of states prohibited non-Protestants from holding public office. Connecticut and Massachusetts were two of several states that had official state churches. It wasn't until the 1940s that the U.S. Supreme Court ruled that state governments also had to uphold the First Amendment's guarantee of religious freedom.

Didn't any of the early settlers believe in freedom of religion?

William Penn, for one, was actually pretty good about such things. He was a member of the Society of Friends (they were called Quakers by their enemies, and the name eventually stuck). The Quakers had been severely persecuted in Europe, and Penn was determined that others shouldn't go through the same ordeal. So he promised freedom of religion in his settlement of "Sylvania." (To Penn's consternation, the king added "Penn's" to the settlement's name when he wrote out the charter. This was in honor of William's father, not William, and of course the king's coinage is still in use today.)

Although Penn was good at granting religious freedom to almost everybody, Roger Williams was even better. As the fiercest defender of religious freedom, Williams almost got himself kicked out of the New World. He and his family came to the Massachusetts Bay Colony in 1631. Williams, however, refused an invitation to become the minister of a Boston church because he opposed its ties to the Church of England. He took on the ruling

Puritans, arguing that the royal charter did not justify taking the Indians' land and that they should not be punishing non-Puritans because of their differences in religion.

In 1636, officials of the Massachusetts Bay Colony attempted to seize the troublemaker and send him back to England, but Williams fled into the wilderness. He decided to start his own colony based on complete religious freedom and fair treatment of the Indians. Unlike most of the colonists, Williams actually bought land from the Natives at a fair price. He founded Providence, Rhode Island, and opened it up to all religions, including some that even Penn couldn't tolerate—Roman Catholics, Jews, and atheists. Because of this radical tolerance, the New England Federation refused to allow the Rhode Island colonies to join for many years.

Where is Roger Williams buried?

Well, funny thing about that. His body was eaten by an apple tree—and we're not kidding. Centuries after his death, the Rhode Island Historical Society wanted to bury him in a better resting place. However, when they dug up his grave, they discovered that Williams was gone, bones and all. An apple tree's roots had entered his coffin near his head and apparently liked what it found. The root grew down his spine, branched out when it got to his arms and legs, and even curved upward into his feet and toes. If you want to see the tree root that ate Roger Williams, you're out of luck. Last time we checked, the Historical Society had it hidden in the basement of the John Brown House in Providence, Rhode Island.

LIVIN' IN AN AMISH PARADISE

What part of Holland did the Pennsylvania Dutch come from?

Germany, actually. It was one of those funny language misunderstandings. When asked what nationality they were, the new settlers said "Deutsch." Americans were never very good with languages.

Were all of the Pennsylvania Dutch Amish?

No. There were also Mennonites, Lutherans, and some other denominations who had heard about Pennsylvania's tradition of religious freedom. By 1790, people of German descent made up about a third of the state's population.

Who founded the Amish, and how did they decide to get stuck in a time warp?

Before there were Amish, there were Mennonites, founded in the 1530s by a Roman Catholic priest named Menno Simons. The Mennonites believed that the Reformation hadn't gone far enough, and so they created their own churches based on the simplicity of Jesus' Sermon on the Mount. As pacifist non-nationalists, they refused to swear oaths, go to war, or even hold an office that might at some time require the use of force. They also didn't believe in baptizing children, feeling that baptism and church membership should be reserved for adults who were mature enough to make a complete commitment to their way of life.

The Amish were a group that splintered off from the Mennonites. They were named for Jacob Ammann who broke away in the 1690s because he thought that even the Mennonites were too worldly. The Amish practice an extreme level of simplicity and disconnection from the rest of the world, including a permanent shunning of any of their members who have failed to live up to their high expectations.

Despite what it looks like to the eyes of outsiders, the Amish time-warp lifestyle was not a deliberate attempt to stay stuck in time, but rather a conscious choice by their elders to live within their professed goals of simplicity, community, and separateness. For example, some Amish use gas-powered refrigerators and solar- and wind-generated electrical power, which is okay because it doesn't require a dependence on the outside world to supply electricity. Several Amish families may share a telephone, which they keep in a barn out of the way. That's okay, because it isn't ringing in their home and distracting them from their lives.

According to one story, early in the 20th century the elders allowed phones in the homes until one woman picked up the party line and heard two neighbors gossiping about her. After that, the elders decided that the telephone—like radios and television in the decades to follow—was a corrosive and divisive influence. Many Amish will accept rides in cars, but will not own them because of the spiritual hazards of having such easy mobility into the world outside. Besides, cars are a status symbol, which can breed jealousy, degrade a sense of equality, and divert people from what really matters spiritually: a simple life with a dependence on God and their community.

If the Amish are so separated from our contemporary world, what was the story a few years back about wild Amish teens driving cars and using drugs?

That's an interesting result of the historic Mennonite/Amish decision that only mature adults should be allowed to become members. For older teens (too old to be ordered around like kids but too immature to commit to membership), there is a peculiar Amish, letting-off-steam institution called *rumschpringes* or "time out." The teens are encouraged to go out, sow a few wild oats, and live a worldly life for a few years until they get it out of their systems and develop some maturity. The teens join "buddy gangs" (with names like the Antiques, the Crickets, and the Pilgrims), buy souped-up cars and stereos, drink, date, go to dances, and otherwise act like teens everywhere.

But isn't that a bad idea? How many would want to go back to barn raisings after being exposed to bikes, burgers, and Britney Spears? Here's where it gets interesting. True, a few may get into serious trouble, and others may decide to leave the Amish community and become Mennonites (or worse!). Still, a surprisingly large proportion of the Amish youth taste the forbidden fruit and decide that it is not as nourishing as the simple life. Besides, the threat of being permanently shunned by friends, family, and community likely makes a decision to leave the church for good a very difficult one.

BRING 'EM PRETTY & BRING 'EM YOUNG

How many wives did Brigham Young have?

Brigham Young became the Mormon leader after church founder Joseph Smith was lynched in 1844. He fervently preached that "plural" marriages were the key to a happy and healthy home. Over the course of his life, Young had 55 wives, some of whom were indeed happy.

From the news, it's obvious that some Mormons still practice polygamy. Was polygamy ever officially outlawed in the Mormon church or is it still acceptable?

Polygamy has been officially against Mormon teachings since 1890, when then church president Wilford Woodruff spoke out against the practice. Since that time, small Mormon church groups have continued to spring up, still actively professing the original polygamous teachings of Joseph Smith and Brigham Young.

Is it true that the Mormon Church used to consummate marriages at the temple during the marriage ceremony?

Although it's an intriguing common bit of anti-Mormon propaganda, it's patently untrue. As with all temple rites, the church holds forth that marriage rites are "sacred, not secret." This was true in the early days of the Mormon Church and in today's temple as well. A Mormon marriage takes place in a room that's reserved only for the administration of marital rites (called a "sealing room"). The ceremony goes something like this: The (fully clothed) man and woman kneel down on a padded altar, not unlike the kneeling altar in Catholic churches, facing one another and holding hands while the priest (also fully clothed) recites vows. This all takes place in less than a minute and culminates in the priest asking the man and woman if they are sure they wish to be wed, asking if either person feels coerced into the union. The priest then blesses the

Ask!

How can I use the Mormon genealogical records to search for my ancestors?

couple, makes wishes for them to spawn many children, and gives them a few quick reminders on how to create a happy marriage. After coming out of the sealing room, the couple exchanges rings and has a picture or two snapped, and that's it. Many modern couples choose to have a more traditional wedding ceremony and reception following the official temple marriage.

LEAVING A DUBIOUS IMPRESSION

Okay, I lost track through all the years of claims and counterclaims. What was the final word on the Shroud of Turin—real, fake, or still unknown?
Fake.

In 1988, carbon dating established that it was made sometime between 1260 and 1380 A.D. This also confirms the first church comment on the matter that was made in 1389 A.D. When the shroud was first displayed by a nobleman, the Bishop of Troyes condemned it as a forgery that had been "cunningly painted" in 1355. He wrote in a memo that his predecessor had actually talked with the artist who created it. In 1389, Pope Clement VII officially declared that the cloth was a painted "representation," nothing more.

The shroud first mysteriously appeared in 1355 in France, displayed by a nobleman named Geoffrey de Charny. He didn't reveal where he'd gotten it. In 1453, Geoffrey's granddaughter sold it to the House of Savoy, a royal family of Italy, conveniently neglecting to mention that the church had already debunked it. The new owners moved it to Italy, and in 1578, began exhibiting it in a special chapel in Turin.

What we do know is that it is one of about forty known relics purported as the "authentic" shroud that covered Jesus' body after his death. It's a particularly good relic. Otherwise intelligent people of our time have been wowed by true believers' claims that the image is a "3-D photographic negative," which *must* have been a miracle because it would've been impossible for medieval folks to know that much about photography.

It's true that they knew nothing about photography, but they *did* know about paints. They knew that if you covered a corpse or statue with finely ground pigment before laying a sheet over it, you will get an effect similar to what is on the Turin shroud. Scientists say this is probably how it was created by that artist in the 14th century.

Yet faith is a mysterious and maddeningly stubborn thing. Even after being pretty thoroughly debunked, some believers continue to grasp at ways that the shroud *could* be genuine, speculating that perhaps the same "miracle" that created the shroud image also threw off the carbon dating. However, to believe that, you have to be able to shrug off the fact that this faulty carbon dating just happened to correlate to the time period when the cloth mysteriously appeared and when a bishop of the church swore on firsthand knowledge that it was painted. That seems like such a coincidence that you'd almost have to consider it some sort of perverse divine intervention. But perhaps God works in mysterious ways.

SAINTS PRESERVE US

I saw the picture of a stained-glass window of a woman carrying her eyeballs on a plate. What's that all about?

That's Saint Lucy. She's the patron saint of the blind. As history tells it, she was a Roman governor who had her eyes put out because of her Christian faith.

Keep your own eye out for these other strange depictions in historical Catholic churches:

- ◆ Saint Rocco, seen with a lesion on his leg and a dog licking it
- ◆ Saint Hedwig, portrayed with shoes under her arm and no shoes on her feet
- ◆ Saint Dymphna, often seen surrounded by crazy people in golden shackles
- ◆ Saint Stanislaus, usually portrayed being chopped up in front of an altar
- ◆ Saint Guignole, a guy with a pronounced erection

THE PAPAL'S CHOICE

Why don't all the Catholic cardinals get to vote for a new pope?

The rules are that cardinals over 80 are not allowed to vote; only 120 cardinals are allowed to vote at one time; and no cardinal under 80 can be excluded from voting. As a practical result, a pope is not allowed to appoint more than 120 men under the age of 80 to the cardinalate.

The voting begins with the death of a pope. The death is verified by a special officer, the *Cardinal Camerlengo*. Traditionally, he does this by standing over the pope's prone body and calling the pope's name loudly three times. If the pope doesn't respond, the camerlengo starts arranging a funeral, nine days of mourning, and an election.

How come we've never heard much about how the voting went when popes were chosen in the past?

The cardinals are commanded to act in complete secrecy, which is taken very seriously. If any of them blab, not only are they threatened with losing their position but also with excommunication from the church.

Traditionally, the pope always had to be elected by a two-thirds majority, but Pope John Paul II has changed that, reportedly to make it easier to elect a doctrinal conservative. Now, after 30 successive but unsuccessful votes, the cardinals can decide to elect the pope by a simple majority. In the past, the two-thirds rule made it likely that the hard-liners in the majority had to come up with a candidate who was also acceptable to the moderates and liberals. Sometimes, when seriously deadlocked, they'd deliberately "punt" the decision forward by nominating an elderly cardinal in poor health with the idea that he'd likely serve a short and uneventful term and die within a few years. This strategy sometimes backfires, however, as with Pope John XXIII, who was 77 when elected but who made major reforms to the church in the five years he served. (Hey, once you're pope, you can pretty much do what you want.)

After each vote the ballots are counted by Vatican clerks, stitched together with a needle and thread, and then burned. If no one gets enough votes, the Vatican staff members add wet straw to the fire to make black smoke, to signal to the outside world that there is not yet a new pope. If a new pope has been chosen, they burn the papers with dry straw to make white smoke.

I WAS A TEENAGE POPE

What was the youngest age of any pope?

Benedict IX—known prior to his post as Theophylactus, and afterward as the Boy Pope—was only about 18 years old when his father essentially bought him the papal seat in 1032. The problem with kids is that they never appreciate what's been given to them: He sold the papacy to his uncle in 1044 as he was fleeing from hostile factions. After things cooled down, Benedict got a case of seller's remorse and forcibly reclaimed the papacy in 1045. He held it for only a month before he lost it again, but the spunky little guy wouldn't give up, reseizing the office again in 1047 before being run out of Rome for good. It's said he died in penitence for his evil deeds at a monastery in 1056. But, not surprisingly, he's not the church's favorite pope.

The oldest pope? A man named Ugolino became Pope Gregory IX at (reportedly) 86 years old in 1227. (However, some historians set his birth date as only "before 1170"; others say "around 1145.") Before his papal appointment, he had a long career as a deeply devoted theologian, diplomat, and lawyer and was said to be close friends with St. Francis of Assisi. He held the office for about 13-and-a-half years, dying at a *really* ripe old age.

IDENTITY CRISIS

Why do all the Pope Stephens have two numbers by them?

Because Stephen II (752 A.D.) died four days after taking office, but before he could be officially consecrated. Because of this, he was left off the official pope charts until 800 years later when church historians decided he belonged there after all. Unfortunately, this caused confusion because eight other

Stephens had held office since his death. Papal scholars assigned a parenthetical second number to each Pope Stephen after Stephen II. In other words, Pope Stephen V then became Pope Stephen V (VI). They hoped that this new system would clarify the situation. Obviously, it hasn't.

DIG YOU LATER

What's the story about the dead pope who was dug up and put on trial?

Ah, yes, the Cadaveric Synod. During the latter part of the ninth century, Pope Formosus made a number of enemies in the various palace intrigues that surrounded the popes of the time. After his death, one of his enemies was elected, Pope Stephen VI (VII).

He had really tried to put the past behind him, but months after becoming pope, Stephen still found himself brooding over the injustices that Formosus had subjected him to. He decided that it was never too late for justice to be served, so he ordered the late pope dug up from his grave, dressed in papal robes, and placed on trial for his sins.

Unfortunately, Formosus wasn't much of a conversationalist by then, and his aides argued that it was unfair that Formosus would not be able to defend himself. Stephen, being a fair man, agreed that they had a point, and so he came up with a solution. He had a junior deacon crouch behind the corpse and answer the charges as if he were the dead pope. According to Richard Zacks in *An Underground Education,* at one point in the trial, "Pope Stephen—a disturbed young man—glowered at the rotting corpse, the skeletal caricature of a pontiff, and shouted: 'Why did you usurp this See of the Apostle?' A teenage deacon, crouched nearby, replied: 'Because I was evil.' "

John Dollison wrote in *Pope-Pourri* that the young deacon actually mounted a fairly credible defense. Even so, the cadaver was found guilty on all counts. "Stephen declared all of Formosus's papal acts null and void. He then chopped off the three fingers on the corpse's right hand used to give blessings; then he had the body stripped naked and dumped in a cemetery for foreigners. A few days later he had the corpse dug up and flung into the Tiber River, where a hermit fished it out and gave it a proper burial."

Stephen VI was tossed into prison not long after and was strangled there. For the next decade or so, popes held synod after synod—some renouncing Stephen's gruesome sentence, and some reinstating it. Finally Pope John IX put an end to the issue with a decree that all trials of dead people were officially prohibited, especially those of popes.

Has there ever been a period of time when there was no pope?

According to the *Catholic Encyclopedia's List of Popes,* there have been several occasions. Usually this was for some political reason, namely infighting among the church bishops themselves, or struggles between the Roman government and the church.

Take, for example, the papal election of 1241. Pope Gregory IX died while struggling for power against the Holy Roman Emperor Frederick II. Roman Senator Matteo Orsini wanted to force the College of Cardinals into picking a pope of his choosing—and quickly—so he had the cardinals locked into a dilapidated Roman temple. The windows were boarded up, there wasn't enough furniture to go around, and only small portions of food were shoved under the door.

Weeks passed, and the cardinals still refused to bend to Orsini's wishes. To pressure them further, Orsini ordered that his guards use the roof's holes as their personal toilets, making the cardinals' meeting room pretty unbearable. When an English cardinal fell sick and died, Orsini refused to take the body away. The body was left in the room with the remaining cardinals.

In the course of 66 days, two more cardinals died from the harsh conditions. Finally, the survivors chose an extremely sick man from their midst, Godfrey of Sabina, as Pope Celestine IV, just to get the process over with. As expected, he died very soon afterward—17 days into the papacy, quite possibly as a result of the ordeal. However, the cardinals were no fools. They absolutely refused to return to Rome to pick a new pope and simply left the office empty for two years.

How many Pope Gregorys were there? Which one invented the Gregorian chant?

So far there've been 16 Pope Gregorys. The first one, Pope St. Gregory the Great, served from 590–604; the last, from 1831–1846. It was the earliest Gregory to whom the Catholics attribute the chanting. However, he didn't really invent it. It's just that the church determined centuries after the fact that at some time during the reign of Gregory I and his successor, Gregory II, a form of musical notation was created to preserve older Roman chants. Because he was pope at the time, the church decided to give him credit.

Incidentally, it was yet another Gregory—Gregory XIII—who, in 1582, commissioned the Gregorian calendar. Not that he actually *invented* the calendar; he merely picked the best proposal submitted to him.

Are popes automatically considered saints?

Pope Gregory VII declared all popes saints, but that fell away not long after Gregory VII died. Pope Stephen V (VI), during the late 800s, self-servingly ruled an even higher papal honor: "The popes, like Jesus, are conceived by their mothers through the overshadowing of the Holy Ghost. All popes are a certain species of man-god. . . . All powers in heaven, as well as on earth are given to them."

Contemporary Catholic thought has it that popes are good candidates for sainthood, but that the process is far from automatic.

YOU SAY YOU WANT A REVOLUTION?

"If you talk about destruction, don't you know that you can count me out . . . in," sang an ambivalent John Lennon in the 1960s. Not everybody has been so undecided throughout history. Some have taken to lopping off governments—and sometimes heads—in the hopes that doing so will somehow make a better world.

GIVE ME LIPTON TEA OR GIVE ME DEATH

Is there a historical marker at the site of the Boston Tea Party?

Yes, there is, and you can read it without getting your feet wet.

Wait a minute, you say. Didn't the Boston Tea Party take place in the middle of Boston Harbor? How could they mount a historical marker there?

Well, never underestimate "progress." The city has filled in so much of what was once the harbor that the actual site of the Tea Party is now well on solid ground. The historical plaque that marks the site is sheepishly mounted along a freeway service road several hundred yards inland from the waterfront. Just head inland from the spurious replica ship that they'd very much like you to believe marks the genuine historical location, and keep your eyes peeled.

Did any famous people take part in the Boston Tea Party?

Historians say that 50 to 100 ruffians disguised as "Indians," complete with hatchets, ash-darkened skin, and war paint, attacked three British merchant ships loaded with tea, hacked open 342 chests of tea, and tossed them overboard into Boston Harbor, one by one. It's believed that brewer-patriot Samuel Adams directed the action but didn't actually dirty his hands with war paint and tea. The most famous name you'd recognize from those who actually boarded the ships with a hatchet? Paul Revere.

Contrast the historians' figure above with that of the Massachusetts Daughters of the American Revolution: The group's website lists no fewer than 168 participants by name. Now it could be that the historians are wrong. It's also possible that the DAR is inflating the figures to expand their membership rolls. More likely, though, as it is with most historical events, more people claimed to have participated than actually did.

How long did the Boston Tea Party take?

There was an awful lot of tea on those three ships. Participants and the mass of eyewitnesses on the shore describe a scene of near-silence interrupted only by the crack of hatchet on wooden crates and the splash of the crates in the water. This was because it was a solemn occasion—they didn't want their voices to be recognized, and they were nervous about raising alarms in the British military vessels within earshot. The revolutionaries made it clear that the tea was the target, so the captains of the ships surrendered with the solemn assurance that nothing else would be damaged. On one ship, a padlock had to be cut to get to the tea, and the next day a messenger delivered a new padlock to replace it. The whole thing took about three hours, and then the faux Indians melted back into the night.

Unfortunately, with the huge quantity of tea and an uncharacteristically still wind, dry tea leaves were still floating on the surface of the harbor when the next morning dawned. Nobody wanted to repeat the troubles of the night before when the mob roughed up people who were caught scavaging tea for their own use, so patriots went out in rowboats and beat the dry tea with the oars until it was sufficiently steeped in the harbor's salty brine.

What were the names of the three tea ships that were boarded during the Boston Tea Party?

The *Dartmouth,* the *Eleanor,* and the *Beaver.*

BEERCENTENNIAL

Was the Samuel Adams Beer Company founded by Samual Adams, the patriot?

I'm sure the company would be happy if you thought so. It's true that signer of the Declaration of Independence, Samuel Adams, was a brewer. However, that was long ago. The Boston Beer Company, which makes the beer that currently bears his name, wasn't founded until 1984.

LISTEN MY CHILDREN, BUT YOU SHAN'T HEAR

If Paul Revere got stopped before finishing his famous ride, why is he still famous?

Maybe it's because "Listen my children and you shall hear / Of the midnight ride of Dr. Samuel Prescott" doesn't rhyme. "Paul Revere's Ride," the famous poem by Henry Wadsworth Longfellow, certainly helped seal Mr. Revere's fame. This, despite the fact that both he and William Dawes got turned back by redcoats before they could reach Concord and wake the minutemen with "The British are coming!" Prescott slipped through the lines, though, and made the hero's ride.

Still, perhaps Revere deserves a poem anyway. He was a trusted courier for secret missions, designed the state seal still used by Massachusetts, built and ran the revolutionaries' gunpowder mill, cast bells and cannons, crafted the copper fittings for the U.S.S. Constitution ("Old Ironsides"), designed and printed the first issue of Continental paper money, and even made false teeth for George Washington. The only thing Revere didn't seem to be any good at was soldiering. In 1779, he was accused of cowardice and insubordination after commanding artillery in the disastrous Penobscot Expedition, which cost nearly all of the Massachusetts trading fleet. A military trial cleared him of wrongdoing in 1782, but he still left military service with his reputation in tatters.

Ask! *Where can I see the route of Paul Revere's famous ride?*

In what battle were the soldiers told to not fire until they saw the whites of the enemies' eyes?

The Battle of Bunker Hill in June 1775. The Americans were running out of ammunition when Colonel William Prescott ordered, "You men are all marksmen, now don't shoot until you can see the whites of their eyes." The strategy worked well in driving back the British soldiers' first two charges. However, on the third charge, the Americans decided that discretion was the better part of valor, etc. They ran.

Where was the Battle of Bunker Hill?

It took place on nearby Breed's Hill, just outside of Boston, Massachusetts.

SUNSHINE PATRIOTS, SUMMERTIME SOLDIERS

Did any signers of the Declaration of Independence have a change of heart and support the king?

Only one: Richard Stockton of Princeton, New Jersey. In fact, he had had qualms about signing the Declaration in the first place but had been swayed by the heady rhetoric at the convention. When captured by the British during the war, he signed an oath of loyalty to the king. However, after the war ended, he changed his mind once again and supported the winning side. Smart man, he.

Did any Americans support King George instead of the revolutionaries?

Quite a few, actually, including many family members of the patriots. For example, Benjamin Franklin's son William sent the authorities secret reports on the activities of his father until he was caught and jailed. Although opinion polls were not a staple of the 18th century, historians say that about a third of the Americans supported the British, about a third supported the American revolutionaries, and the rest just wished everybody would shut up and stop fighting. We do know that more American residents joined the (pro-British) loyalist army than the (anti-British) continental army.

How much did the British pay their mercenary Hessian soldiers from Germany?

About twenty-five cents a day—less than three dollars in today's money.

FREEDOM FIGHTERS

Were the slaves who fought in the Revolutionary War freed?

Those who fought for the British, yes, but not the ones who fought for the patriots. In fact, many southern slaveholders didn't actively fight against the British for freedom because they were afraid that their slaves might get inspired to do the same thing.

British recruiters in Virginia augmented their fighting forces by making an offer that few slaves would want to refuse: "Fight on our side, and we'll free you after the war." About 2,000 slaves took them up on it, including 22 who escaped from the Monticello estate of Thomas Jefferson.

After the war started winding down, most of the freed slaves found it wise to move to Canada; some joined an expedition to Africa to found the country of Sierra Leone.

FLOGGING THE CAUSE OF FREEDOM

What did old navy man "I Have Not Yet Begun to Fight" John Paul Jones do after the revolution ended?

Well, he certainly didn't stick around on land for long, savoring his victories. That was partly because he had been a seafarin' guy since the age of 12. That, and there was always a chance that a couple of old murder charges might surface and cause him some trouble.

The man who would later be called "the Father of the American Navy" was born a Scot in 1747 and had been captaining merchant ships across the Atlantic since the age of 22. Jones's real name was simply John Paul. He didn't add "Jones" until 1773. He did so to hide his identity when he became a fugitive from justice. It turns out he had killed two sailors under his command—one by flogging, another during what he insisted was a mutiny attempt—and had been charged with murder in both cases.

When the American Revolution began, the patriots had a shortage of skilled captains to challenge the British at sea. Jones saw his chance to go back to sea without running the risk of being asked too many questions about his past.

During the war, Jones and his crew fought bravely and skillfully. One time they captured a better-armed British ship by pulling up alongside it and engaging its crew in three hours of hand-to-hand combat.

After the war, though, a move to promote Jones to rear admiral was scuttled, and the American navy was decommissioned. By 1787, Jones was casting around for a new job. Empress Catherine of Russia had heard of his bravery and sent him a flattering offer, asking him to serve as a rear admiral in her Black Seas fleet, which was fighting the Turks.

Unfortunately, his service there was hampered by jealousy from the Russian officers, language difficulties, and a resurgence in his difficulties at building nurturing subordinate relationships. After two years he retired from the Russian Navy and went to live in France. While he was there, the U.S. government appointed Jones commissioner to Algiers, but Jones died at age 45 before news of the appointment made it across the ocean to him.

Here's an ironic, posthumous ending: A century later, in 1905, Jones was nominated for the Hall of Fame for Great Americans in New York City, but the nomination was rejected—not because of the two murder charges, but because of his service in the Russian Navy. He was finally elected in 1925.

ONE IF BY LAND

What was General George Washington's horse named during the war?

He had several, but he mostly rode "Nelson" and "Blueskin."

Who did King George III call "an evil genius"?
Benjamin Franklin.

Was Washington ever shot?

On two different occasions, enemy marksmen shot through his coat and hat, but fortunately, not through Washington himself.

FIGHTING TIGERS

How many times did Princeton University change hands during the Revolutionary War?

Nassau Hall, the main structure of what would become Princeton University, was captured and recaptured three times during the heat of battle. Finally, British soldiers made their last stand there before American artillery convinced them to surrender (doing quite a bit of damage to the building and its furnishings in the process, it should be noted). The battle ended with an American victory on January 3, 1777. At the time, the school was called the College of New Jersey. The school had been chartered 30 years earlier by King George II as a Presbyterian school "for the Education of Youth in the Learned Languages and in the Liberal Arts and Sciences," the fourth university chartered in the British colonies (after Harvard, William and Mary, and Yale). Coincidentally, the college president at the time was the Reverend John Witherspoon, one of the signers of the Declaration of Independence. Classes continued after the battle ended, and the Class of '77 boasted a record number of graduates—30, up from 27 in 1776.

THE FAT LADY SINGS

What was the name of the song played at the surrender of the British to the Americans at Yorktown?

None of the accounts at the time identified a tune, but about fifty years after the fact, a legend developed that it was "a well known song" called "The World Turned Upside Down." The title is so fitting to the situation that people assume it must be true, but the evidence is pretty dubious. Most likely, they played a variety of slow marches because the process of surrendering—marching forward in a line and dropping their weapons into a pile—took quite a bit of time.

Ask! Where can I hear music from the American Revolution?

YOU WENT THE WRONG WAY, OLD KING LOUIE

Did the American Revolution inspire the French Revolution?

In more ways than you might imagine. The obvious link was that the heady concepts of freedom and equality traveled well over the ocean. The less obvious connection was that King Louis XVI actually helped finance the American rebels, figuring that any enemy of England was a friend of his. Perhaps he should've listened more carefully to the Americans' anti-king rhetoric before he laid his money down. Most certainly, he should've consulted his treasurer because his aid to the Americans badly depleted his treasury. He ended up raising taxes on the already-struggling peasantry and middle class. After that, it didn't take much to light the fire of revolution.

NOTHING SAYS LOVIN' LIKE SOMETHING FROM THE OVEN

Why did Marie Antoinette say, "Let them eat cake"?

The story suggests Antoinette was not sympathetic to the hungry plight of the French population. As it's told, someone explained to Queen Marie that the people had no bread and she replied offhandedly, "Let them eat cake."

However, a little digging suggests that Marie Antoinette was never that coldhearted or ignorant of her people's suffering. It turns out that the "let them eat cake" incident was recorded in Jacques Rousseau's *Confessions,* published in 1781, quoting a Grenoble princess in 1740. French revolutionaries borrowed the story and attributed it to the queen, who wasn't even born until 1755, in an attempt to sully her name. It worked.

A GIRL'S BEST FRIEND

Did Marie Antoinette ever wear the Hope Diamond?

Yes. It was part of France's collection of crown jewels. After the revolution, they were looted, and the diamond disappeared. When it reappeared twenty years later, it had been cut from 67 carats down to 45 to disguise its origins. What happened to the missing piece or pieces nobody seems to know, but what's left of the Hope Diamond is now in the Smithsonian in Washington, D.C.

GET OUT OF JAIL FREE

How many prisoners were released when the French revolutionaries tore down the Bastille?

The Bastille housed personal and political prisoners of the king and queen. Voltaire and the Marquis de Sade had both been alumni. The number of people incarcerated there varied widely at any given time. On July 14, 1789, the prison population was at a low swing. When hundreds of howling peasants overpowered the prison's guards, they discovered only seven captives there to liberate, and none of them were political prisoners. Even worse, the revolutionaries didn't find a cache of weapons to liberate either, as they had hoped. Oh, well, at least they got to keep all the souvenir rubble they could carry. It'd probably be worth something today on eBay.

HEADS WILL ROLL

Do we have any idea how many people were beheaded during the French Revolution?

The rabble didn't keep great records, but it was something like 17,000 beheadings. Only 30% of the executed were aristocrats and landowners—the bulk of them were peasants being punished for draft-dodging and other crimes against the revolution. Another 23,000 people died in prison or battle, their heads still attached to their bodies.

What were Marie Antoinette's last words?

Before Marie Antoinette's execution, she was paraded through the city in a wooden cart, where she was mocked and spat upon by the crowds for three hours. As she ascended the platform to the guillotine, she accidentally stepped on the executioner's foot. Her last words were "I am sorry, Monsieur. It was not intentional."

Did the head of Marie Antoinette blush after she was executed?

According to legend, after Marie Antoinette's beheading, the executioner lifted her severed head and slapped her face, which blushed a bright red. However, this is probably unlikely, considering how much blushing is dependent on blood moving through veins. In fact, witnesses to other beheadings described the victim's face as immediately drained of color, then turning ashen and waxy. If there is any truth to the story at all, it could be that her rouge suddenly stood out in sharp contrast to her ashen skin, giving the impression of a blush.

Is it true that Dr. Guillotine became the victim of his invention during the French Revolution?

No, it's a myth. His connection with the death machine cost him much remorse, but not his life.

Dr. Joseph Guillotin was a humanitarian. He did not invent the machine that came to bear his name; he did, however, lobby the French government to adopt a "humane" method of executing criminals.

Up until that time, beheading was even more gruesome than most people could ever imagine. Executioners often missed chopping the head off cleanly the first time, leading to the excruciating spectacle of victims bleeding and howling in great pain while he tried again (and sometimes again and again) to get it right. The prospect was bad enough that some condemned prisoners paid the executioner a gratuity before kneeling at the block to encourage him to sharpen his blade, aim true, and make death as quick and painless as possible.

Guillotin's lobbying paid off. The government eventually decided to use the fast, foolproof design that now bears its sponsor's name. Unfortunately, this decision took place just before the revolution's Reign of Terror. The revolutionary council loved the new machine not because it was humane, but because it was efficient. They could dispatch hundreds of people in a day at breakneck speed (no pun intended). Although Guillotin was not one of them, he was described as "inconsolable" for the rest of his life in that he felt somewhat responsible for the bloodletting that took place during that time. "He had aimed at relieving the sufferings of the culprits condemned by severe but just laws," wrote a biographer, "but he unintentionally contributed to the destruction of a greater number of human beings. [He believed that] had they been put to death in a less expeditious manner, the people might have soon been wearied out by those executions."

Years later, Guillotin's descendents tried to get the French government to change the name of the killing device. When that didn't work, they gave up and decided to change the family name.

Can a head live after being severed by a guillotine, and for how long?

It's a good question. Good enough that a scientist who had been condemned to the guillotine during the French Revolution decided to try to settle the issue once and for all. Chemist Antoine Lavoisier was one of France's greatest scientists. He discovered oxygen and helped lay the groundwork for modern chemistry. Then he ran afoul of the French revolutionary government and was sentenced to death. Lavoisier had heard stories of disembodied heads saying prayers, looking around, and otherwise showing signs of life for short periods after decapitation. Ever the scientist, he decided that as his last experiment, he would try to demonstrate whether a head could continue to be alive after beheading, and for how long. He told a friend, "Watch my eyes after the blade comes down. I will continue blinking as long as I retain consciousness." The results of the experiment? Lavoisier blinked for about 15 seconds.

CITIZENS! CURFEW AT 9:80 SHARP!

Is it true that the Revolutionary government used a ten-hour metric clock?

Yes. After they won, the revolutionaries began a reign of terror in which they forced the population to convert to the horrors of metric measurement. Most people don't know that the post-revolutionary French invented the metric system most of the world now uses for measuring weight, volume, and distance.

But that wasn't enough for those wild-eyed radicals. They decided to replace the 60-minute/24-hour clock with a metric clock, and the seven-day week with a ten-day week, which they called a "decade." People worked for nine days and took the tenth day as a day of rest. Each day was divided into ten metric hours of 100 metric minutes, and each metric minute consisted of 100 metric seconds. The whole system was confusing, and people quickly caught on that they were getting fewer rest days than in a seven-day week. After trying it out and finding it too disconcerting for most people, the government abandoned metric time.

FOOLS RUSSIAN

American troops were already fighting near Russia during World War I, so why didn't they intervene to stop the Communists from taking over Russia and save a lot of trouble in the 20th century?

It's a little-known fact, but Woodrow Wilson *did* send American forces in to help the White Russians (royalists loyal to the czarist system). Along with a force of Japanese, who had long been an enemy of the Russians, American soldiers fought for two years before being forced to flee the country in 1920. Unfortunately, the intervention by Americans didn't turn the tide of battle, and it helped convince the Russians that the Americans were not to be trusted, setting the stage for mutual, bitter antagonism for the rest of the century.

After the Bolshevik leaders were exiled from Russia, how did they get back in?

Germany smuggled them back in, figuring it was the easiest way of getting Russia out of World War I. Even though Czar Nicholas had abdicated, the provisional government that took over continued fighting in World War I.

Sowing seeds of trouble that they'd have reason to regret for decades afterward, the Germans decided that throwing the Bolsheviks back into the mix would be a good way to keep Russia destabilized. The Germans commissioned a special train to take Lenin and thirty-two other Bolsheviks to Petrograd hoping they would act, as Winston Churchill put it later, "like a typhoid bacillus." The tactic worked. When the Bolsheviks seized power, they signed a peace treaty with Germany in which Russia granted huge concessions. However, the last laugh was on them— Germany continued to drive forward into their territories despite the treaty, capturing huge chunks of land, and the Russian army was too weak from the revolution to resist.

Why does my almanac list Russia's October Revolution as happening in November?

It's true. On November 7, workers, soldiers, and sailors led by the Bolsheviks took over the Winter Palace—the headquarters of the provisional government—and formed a new government headed by Lenin. The Russians call it the October Revolution because to them it was still October. Although most of the world had switched over to the more accurate Gregorian calendar, Russia was still using the old Julian calendar, and the Julian Calendar said it was October 25, by gum.

Why didn't they switch over when the rest of Europe did? It was in large part because of professional jealousy: The Gregorian calendar had been sponsored by a Roman Catholic pope (see page 199). As a result, the Orthodox Russian Catholic Church dragged its feet and was reluctant to embrace it. Turkey was a similar holdout. Finally, though, both countries adopted the Gregorian calendar in the 1920s.

Was Red Square named in honor of the Communists?

No. The park in downtown Moscow has had the same name since a century before the Bolshevik Revolution. But here's the interesting thing: it got its name from a Russian word that could be translated as either "beautiful" or "red," but time, dubious translations, and the Russian Revolution have fixed the name as Red Square in our minds.

MAO & THEN

Was Mao Zedong a spoiled rich kid?

No, he was a legitimate revolutionary, not a dilettante, and was born from true peasant stock. He became radicalized while reading on the job as a library clerk at the National University in Beijing.

How long was Mao's Long March?

Longer than you'd want to walk, most likely. Especially while being bombarded by Chiang Kai-shek's air force. The Long March was a very long, slow retreat by the Chinese communist revolutionaries from southwest China to northeast China, in which they escaped encirclement and hiked 6,000 miles, a little more than the distance from New York to San Francisco and back again. About 100,000 people started walking in October of 1934 near the Kiangsi-Fukien border; about 8,000 were still walking when they arrived in Shensi in October 1935.

Most of the missing people at the end had died from fighting, disease, or starvation, including Mao's two children and younger brother.

Ask! Is Mao's Little Red Book online?

HEROES OF OUR GLORIOUS EVOLUTION

How many people died to win the Canadians their independence?

No Canadian was harmed in the making of that oh-so-reasonable nation. With more of a polite cough than a shot heard 'round the world, Canada's national status was granted in 1931. There was no bloodshed, just a favorable vote by the British Parliament.

THE ORIENT EXPRESSED

It's staggering how far back in time Asian civilization goes and what a wide variety of cultures Asia has encompassed. Yet westerners still know so little of it. With so much to learn and so little time, let's get started. Here's a sampling of the more intriguing questions gleaned from the many received at "Ask Jeeves."

WHAT WILL THEY THINK OF NEXT?

When's the first recorded use of paper in China?

Sometime around 100 A.D. It was made of hemp, and its inventor is supposedly a man named Cai Lun. There's evidence now, however, that there were some forerunners to this hemp paper in China, even before that point.

Did the Chinese invent chinese checkers?

Sorry, no. Its first form hit the gaming scene sometime during the 1880s. It was invented in Victorian England, not China, and was called halma. Not long after, the Germans rearranged the shape of the halma board into a star and sold it as Stern-Halma. A few years later it was imported into the U.S. under the exotic name *Chinese checkers*.

How were firecrackers invented?

Totally by accident. Thousands of years ago, it's speculated, some unsuspecting peasant in China ran out of wood for his fire and decided to pull down some bamboo and use it to keep his blaze going. Surprisingly, when the fire heated the green bamboo, the air and sap inside boiled and pressurized the reeds' empty chambers, causing the sections to explode. This terrifying event led to a wave of religious uses: The loud banging of the exploding bamboo was said to frighten away evil spirits from harvests, weddings, shop openings, and funerals. A tradition was born.

When the Chinese discovered gunpowder—according to some early Taoist alchemy books, perhaps as early as 1,500 years ago— it was only a few hundred years before chemists were able to figure out how to channel that energy into weapons. Once this was done for weapons, figuring out how to pour it into casings that pop and explode was only a small leap away, thus replacing bamboo. The bamboo origins live on, however. To this day, the Chinese name for firecrackers is *pao chuk*. Translated, that's "burst bamboo."

What was the first material in ancient times used to make Chinese jump ropes?

The Chinese jump rope isn't really Chinese at all. It's probably Greek. The truth of the matter is that the origin of this game is recent but relatively unclear. The game reached its height of popularity during the 1970s on playgrounds all over the globe. The materials that were generally used were either rubber bands, connected to one another in a long circle, or a long piece of elastic sewn together.

Regular jump ropes were first documented in China about 1,500 years ago. However, most agree that some form of jump rope had likely existed long before then. Probably about as long ago as the invention of the rope met up with energetic children; some time in the Stone Age.

Who really invented spaghetti: the Chinese or the Italians?

From all indications, they both did. And it seems that many other cultures around the world invented noodles independent of outside influence as well. The popular story, of course, is that Marco Polo brought pasta back from his trips to China sometime around 1295. However, Italian records from a decade earlier indicate that ravioli was a favorite dish of the Romans, years before Marco's return. And fettuccini's history predated ravioli's for certain. This doesn't mean that pasta was found in Italy before it was being consumed in China. The reverse is probably true: At least 3,000 years ago, the Chinese were making pasta out of bean and rice flour. But Italy likely developed the dish without any help from China.

What's the oldest restaurant in the world?

The world's longest-running restaurant is Ma Yu Ching's Bucket Chicken House, opened for business during the Sung dynasty in 1153. It still serves noodles and rice in the city of Kaifeng.

When did the Chinese first use chopsticks?

No one knows a time or date, but it certainly was a long time ago: Most likely when the first person was cooking the first slab of meat in a fire and needed something—a twig or stick—to pull it out.

Chopsticks are first mentioned in a book called *Liji* (the Book of Rites), which was written around 2,000 years ago. But historians seem certain that they had been in existence for thousands of years prior to the publication of that first reference.

DRIP, DRIP, DRIP

Is it true that a person really went crazy when subjected to the ancient practice of Chinese water torture?

If you're talking about constantly dripping water, there's no evidence that the technique was ever really used except in B-grade spy movies. However, other water tortures were used in China.

With the real Chinese water torture, the victim had his hands tied behind his back and his head submerged in water for various lengths of time. Some variations were used: A torturer could alternate dipping the victim's head in scalding-hot and then ice-cold water until the victim either spills the beans or dies.

Yet another variation is to place a water-soaked cloth over the victim's face, lay him on his back, and pour water over his face until he drowns—or comes close to it, anyway.

The truth, however, is that these methods are no more strictly Chinese than spaghetti is. Just about every culture that's employed torture through the ages has used these methods or ones very similar. Maybe the Chinese invented these methods first, as they have so many other things, but probably not.

PASSING THE T'ANG (OR THE SUNG OR THE MING)

Was succession for Chinese emperors always given to the first-born son?

Yes. Placing the first-born son on the throne was of utmost importance in Chinese culture where ancestor worship was practiced. If the lineage was faulty, how could the emperor keep the balance between heaven and the kingdom equalized? It became the practice, starting thousands of years ago, to keep teams of eunuchs around the women's quarters, to make sure the ladies weren't having sex with other males. In times of high infant mortality rates, procreating with the wives and concubines helped guarantee an heir to the throne. The wives got first dibs, lineage-wise, but if none of the wives had sons, the heir apparent came from the concubines' sons.

It's a system that usually worked just fine; however, there have been exceptions. A new dynasty was often started as a result of rebellions and uprisings. The various dynasties were not related to one another. The Ming dynasty's first emperor, for instance, was from a lower-class peasant background; he was not a relative of the noble class. He happened to be the leader of a fairly strong rebellion, and his lineage lasted for about three centuries.

ROYAL PAINS

Were Chinese imperial eunuchs sensitive about their shortcomings?

They had that reputation, yes. Common derogatory nicknames for eunuchs such as Old Rooster or Old Earl were never actually spoken in front of a eunuch, only behind their backs. Furthermore, it was considered bad etiquette to mention things like a tailless dog or a teapot without a spout in the presence of a eunuch, knowing that he might see it as a slight against him about his condition.

What was involved in performing an official kowtow to the emperor?

In China, the kowtow-ee first had to sink to his knees and fall prostrate toward the emperor. Knocking his head nine times on the floor, he could then either lie prostrate with hands on the ground or could sit more upright, but with his eyes and head lowered to the ground. Either way, the emperor was never to be looked at.

Was there any one person or dynasty responsible for the idea of bound feet? Why would they do this?

The story is somewhat based on speculation, as no known origin exists for the practice. But some historians believe the following version to be the most plausible.

There was once a prince who lived about 1,000 years ago. His name was Prince Li Yu, and he ruled one of the Ten Kingdoms of China. He had many wives and concubines, but his favorite was a dancer that he named Precious Thing. She danced for him on a lotus-shaped platform. She also danced inside a six-foot-tall lotus flower made of gold. She laced her feet and calves in silk ribbons to make her dance more seductive. Prince Li Yu loved her very much and approved of this type of dancing, which is similar to what the western world would call en pointe ballet dancing.

It's believed by some that this was a trend-setting moment in Chinese history; that dancers began to misshape their feet to achieve this look, instead of simply dancing on one's toes while wearing hard-toed shoes. All but the first toe were pulled underneath the foot, while bindings forced the heel and the ball of the foot as close together as possible, completely breaking the arch. Within fancy, silk-embroideried shoes, the deformity made women's feet look tiny, as if they were walking on dainty little points. They were dainty, for the few steps they could manage taking, anyway.

From dancers to the nobility, and finally working its way down to the lowest of the socioeconomic classes, the crippling trend was inextricable from Chinese culture by the 17th century. It took the Communist Revolution in the mid-20th century to eventually eradicate the practice entirely.

PORCELAIN GODS

Why are they called Ming vases? Was Ming the artist?

No. It was because the rise in availability and popularity of porcelain goods reached its peak during the Ming dynasty (1368–1644 A.D.). During this period, the kilns at Jingdezhen (the porcelain capital of China) were able to produce large amounts of high-quality porcelain to readily provide all of China with vases, bowls, urns, and other goods. Popular styles included red monochrome vases, yellow imperial bowls, and the detailed, enameled pieces with traditional patterns on them. This is the era that produced so much blue and white porcelain, it found its way to distant shores and became the inspiration for Holland's Dutch delftware patterns. Other industries, like cotton and silk weaving, flourished during the Ming dynasty period as well.

Was the Gate of Heavenly Peace part of the Great Wall?

No, it's the main entrance gate leading to the Imperial (or Forbidden) City. It is pronounced *Tian 'Anmen* in Chinese and is located on the edge of Tiananmen Square in Beijing.

"THIS IS A GREAT WALL"

Who built the Great Wall?

Small sections existed prior to 221 B.C., but we have no known record of who built them or how they came to be. However, we can be certain who is responsible for connecting those small pieces and forming the one long barrier. His name was Emperor Shihuangdi, first emperor of the Qin dynasty. In an effort to block out invading nomadic tribes, he ordered that the wall be built. Construction started in 221 B.C. and concluded in 204 B.C. Each subsequent dynasty continued the tradition of guarding the wall and keeping it repaired. Bits and pieces were added, slowly extending the length over time, but the basic structure remained the same throughout the centuries until the Ming dynasty (1368–1644 A.D.). Redesign and refortification was undertaken during this time, and the wall extended for thousands of more miles into what we see today. As a result, there now exists a wall that runs 4,500 miles and extends from the Korean mountains to the Gobi Desert.

How did the Chinese make the Great Wall so long?

Initially, it was by working thousands of people for a total of seventeen straight years. Many parts of the wall cover mass graves of the workers who died while building it. And it didn't stop with the Qin dynasty. For hundreds of more years, peasants, soldiers, prisoners of war, or criminals were pressed into working on the wall. There are terrible stories of hardships endured by the workers, living with extreme weather and under cruel circumstances. Most knew that if you were picked to work on the wall, there was a good chance you'd never return home. That's the basis for one of China's most well-known, historical poems. It was written in the first or second century by the poet Ch'en Lin, and it's titled "Song: I Watered My Horse at the Long Wall Caves."

Here are some parts of the poem from a translation from *The Columbia Book of Chinese Poetry:*

> *I went and spoke to the Long Wall boss:*
> *"We're soldiers from Taiyuan—will you keep us here*
> *forever?"*
> *"Public works go according to schedule—*
> *swing your hammer, pitch your voice in with the rest!"*
> *A man'd be better off to die in battle*
> *Than eat his heart out building the Long Wall! . . .*
> *I sent a letter to my wife:*
> *"Better remarry than wait any*
> *longer—*
> *serve your new mother-in-law*
> *with care*
> *and sometimes remember the*
> *husband you once had."*

How do I sign up for the Great Wall marathon?

CHINESE CHARACTERS

Why are there two different spoken Chinese languages but only one written one?

There are more than two different spoken Chinese dialects. Most villages and towns throughout China developed their own style of pronunciation and ways of communicating. Therefore, there are several general areas of dialects, and depending on how you want to categorize them, hundreds of variations on these. Some of the main ones include Mandarin, Jin, Cantonese, Gan, Xiang, Min, Hakka, and Wu. But thankfully, there is but one written language, making it possible for any literate Chinese to communicate with any other literate Chinese despite existing language barriers. The reason the written form has remained is primarily because it isn't a phonetic written language, like most other languages, but a pictorial language. Each character in the Chinese written language is a picture, and each picture represents a word. In theory, that word can be pronounced any way you'd like; the picture will always mean the same thing.

Although the written language has been simplified and streamlined over the years, it has remained largely unchanged and continues to offer a communication bridge—a unifying link— in a single country vast enough to have developed so many different spoken tongues.

Does "genghis" mean anything in Chinese?

Yes, it means "precious warrior" in Chinese and is pronounced *cheng-sze*. Genghis Kahn (originally named Temujin) ruled a huge empire that spread across China and throughout Asia and Russia. The Turkish part of his empire dubbed him *kahn*, meaning "lord," and the combination of the two names stuck.

How was Kublai Kahn related to Genghis?

Kublai (prounounced "koo-*bill*-eye," not "koo-blah") was Genghis's grandson.

JAPANESE CHARACTERS

Who was the first ruler of Japan? A Chinese emperor?

Not according to Japanese history books. The first recorded ruler of Japan was a woman: Empress Himoko. She reigned during the fourth century B.C.

Who called himself "the crazy painter"?

Katsushika Hokusai, the famous 19th-century Japanese landscape artist. He changed his name more than 30 times in his 89 years and reportedly lived in 93 different dwellings throughout his life. Clearly, he was a man of change, reshaping himself and his work many times during his career. He is probably the most well known of all Japanese artists, and he found inspiration in Western art forms that, through Dutch trading, were filtering into Japan at the time. Western artists, in turn, had a great respect for Hokusai's work. Impressionists, the likes of Henri Toulouse-Lautrec, Claude Monet, and Edgar Degas, were collectors and were deeply influenced by him. Hokusai was most prolific; it is thought that he produced more than 30,000 pieces during his lifetime. His last words, it is said, were, "If heaven gives me ten more years, or an extension of even five years, I shall surely become a true artist."

THE SOUTH SHALL RISE AGAIN

Was Vietnam ever a part of China?

Vietnam was a vassal state of China for about a millennium, up until around the 10th century. That part of history has produced some bad feelings between the two countries over the years—not unlike any area that achieves independence from a long-standing mother country. However, the Chinese haven't helped the relationship much: The derogatory term *Annam* is still sometimes used by the Chinese when referring to Vietnam. It means "the pacified South," implying a connection to China, despite their longstanding millennium of separation.

GETTING TO KNOW YOU

What was the name of the emperor who's in the story **The King and I?**

His name was Mongkut. In real life he was most known for his skillful negotiations with the British in securing Thailand's—then Siam's—status of self-rule. Few people know, however, that he was also a monk prior to taking the throne and in fact founded the Thammayut Buddhist sect.

How much of The King and I *was actually true?*

Most historians believe it is largely inaccurate, and we're not just talking about the snappy tunes. It is true that Anna Leonowens was the teacher to the King of Siam's wives and children. Fortunately, for readers and moviegoers, the King's son didn't invite Leonowens back to Siam when he took over the throne, so she made a new life as a writer. Her stories were compelling and exotic to English readers, and they sold well. The country of Thailand, however, was offended because of their inaccuracy and lack of respect for their monarchy. The books, movies, play, and the short-lived TV show, all based on Leonowens' personal accounts, are still banned there.

THE CITY OF ANGELS

What does "Bangkok" mean? 'Cause it sounds dirty.

The name Bangkok began appearing on western navigational charts as early as the 1400s. It may have been the Chinese who coined the name originally. By some accounts, the name Bangkok means "village of the wild plum."

So why did westerners go by the Chinese name instead of the Thai name? Well, there was a problem: The real name wouldn't fit on their charts, for one. The official Thai name of the capital city is Krungthep Mahanakorn Amorn Ratanakosin Mahintara Yuthaya Mahadilokpop Noparat Rajathani Burirom Udom Rajaniwej Mahasatarn Amornpimarn Avatarn Satit Saka Tat Tiya Visanu Kumprasit. (Translation: The land of angels, the great city [of] immortality, of various devine gems, the great angelic land unconquerable, land of nine noble gems, the royal city, the pleasant capital, place of the grand royal palace, forever land of angels and reincarnated spirits, predestined and created by the highest Deva[s].) Thankfully, it's usually shorted to *Krung Thep,* which means "City of Angels."

Which country has the Emerald Buddha? Is it made of pure emerald?

The Emerald Buddha (*Wat Phra Keo*) is in Bangkok, Thailand, at the Emerald Buddha Temple (*Wat Phra Rattanasatsadaram*). It's carved from one solid piece of green jade. No one knows who made it or what country it actually came from originally. Many believe it originated in India, many centuries ago, before it surfaced more permanently in northern Thailand about 600 years ago.

HEY, JAKARTA NICE SET-A MOLUCCAS, BABY

What was the first modern-day city in Southeast Asia to hit a population of one million people?

Jakarta, Indonesia. It reached that mark in the mid-1900s, around the same time Indonesia gained independence. It's still one of the 17 largest cities in the world, with a population of over nine million.

Where does nutmeg grow?

The Spice Islands, or the Moluccas, have been a much-sought territory for its cultivation of both nutmeg and cloves since at least the fourth century B.C. Almost every major civilization has fought for the rights to rule there: the Chinese, Dutch, Indian, Portuguese, and Arabs, for instance. In the 1500s, because of the constant battling, it earned the title *Jazirat-al-Muluk* or "Land of Many Kings."

By the early 1800s, nutmeg and clove plantations in Africa began to flourish. They forced the price of the spices down, and the bloody battling for control over the string of Spice Islands declined.

HEY, HEY, WE'RE THE MONKS!

Why do eastern religious monks wear yellow robes?

Only some of them do. There are many Buddhist sects, and each one has different rules governing the color of their dress. The

Mahayanist monks of Vietnam wear brown, the Theravada monks wear dark saffron or yellow. Confucius's followers were told to wear primary colors like yellow, blue, white, black, and red, rather than "intermediate" colors, such as purple or brownish tones. Although red was approved, Confucius personally felt red was for women only.

Taoist monks traditionally opt for yellow robes, following the old Yellow Turban movement of the third century: Priests and missionaries wore yellow robes, and their followers wore yellow turbans simply to distinguish themselves as Taoists.

Alternately, Japanese Shinto priests are limited to only wearing white, light blue, or purple, depending on their rank.

NOT TO BE CONFUSED WITH MOON PIES

Which Chinese festival has "moon cakes"?

They are eaten during the annual Mid-Autumn Festival, a celebration honoring the cycles of the moon and the bounty of the harvest. The words "moon" and "unity" in Chinese are the same word. The Chinese have an old saying: *"Yua yuan ren tuan yuan,"* literally: "When moon forms a circle, people unite." Much like the American Thanksgiving, it's been the traditional time for getting together with family and loved ones. The moon cakes that are eaten during this celebration are paste-filled "cakes" that more resemble pies in the texture of their crusts. The fillings come in a variety of flavors, such as bean paste, melon, duck egg, and minced meats, the most popular being lotus seed paste. Even though the specific traditions have changed somewhat over the years, the little cakes have been eaten since about 300 A.D.

NOT JUST A DISNEY BLOND

Was the Disney movie Mulan *based on a real person?*

The story is based on a poem written by a woman that dates as far back as at least 420 A.D., when the northern kingdoms of China were at constant war with the northern nomadic tribes. The poem was written into a song about a thousand years ago. It is this "Ballad of Mulan" that has been popular among Chinese girls for generations and has laid the groundwork for Disney's plot. However, there is no evidence that Mulan really existed.

Ask! Where can I read the "Ballad of Mulan"?

DOPE PEDDLERS OF THE EMPIRE

Who wanted the opium in the Opium War?

The British. Actually, that's not the entire truth. They didn't *want* the opium *per se;* they wanted the freedom to sell their opium to millions of Chinese. That's the great thing about addicts: They make good customers. The British weren't the only ones to profit from the opium trade: the Americans also did, as well as the Turks and Indians.

China blockaded the British from dealing opium in Canton. The Chinese government had grown weary of watching westerners turn a profit by addicting their countrymen to the potent (and then illegal) drug. They seized all of the British opium in 1839 from Cantonese warehouses, refused to apologize, forbad all trade with Britain, then fired on British warships in their waters. Well, British honor wouldn't allow this effrontery. In retaliation, the British seized Hong Kong and bombed Canton. Finally, China agreed to pay reparations, gave Hong Kong to the British, and reopened several ports to British trade again. This 1842 agreement was called the Treaty of Nanking. As for the British side of the deal, they got to continue to addict millions more of the Chinese, rake in the profits, and have access and trade with

China at no extra cost. As a result, other western countries followed suit, securing similar open and free rights to residence and trade within China's borders. This time period is referred to by the Chinese as "the time of unequal treaties," as they continuously lost control over their own country to stronger western countries like Great Britain, France, Russia, and the United States.

CIVIL
RIGHTS &
WRONGS

History isn't always pretty.

YOU HAVE TO DRAW THE LINE SOMEWHERE

Where did the Mason–Dixon Line get its name?
The line that ended up symbolically delineating the border
between the North and South was named after two British

surveyors who were hired to settle a boundary dispute between Pennsylvania and Maryland in the 1760s. Charles Mason and Jeremiah Dixon were astronomers by training, but their line proved to be more accurate than most surveyors' lines of the time.

Although their east-to-west line marked the boundary between free states and slave states, their north-to-south line, set up at the same time, didn't quite have the same symbolic impact: It ended up being the boundary between Maryland and Delaware.

How many Southerners actually owned slaves when the Civil War began?

Fewer than one in five. Of these, most owned one or two slaves. About 8,000 land owners—fewer than one in a thousand of the people living in slave states—owned 50 or more.

Which state was the last to abolish slavery?

Mississippi. No, not in 1865, but in 1995. While slavery obviously wasn't practiced up until this date (because federal laws supersede state laws on this issue), it took this long for the laws to be officially changed in their state books.

Ask!
Did slaves build the White House and the Capitol?

EVIL IN THE HEARTS OF MEN

How many people were lynched in the United States?

From 1889 through 1930, at least 3,724 people were lynched. About 80% were black, and nearly all of the lynchers were white. Some of the victims were merely hung; others were burned alive; and some were tortured hideously with castration and dismemberment first. Even though the lynchmen were easily recognized in photos sometimes proudly printed up as postcards afterward, few lynchers were ever arrested or prosecuted.

Was the Oklahoma bombing the worst act of terrorism in the United States in the 20th century?

In the twentieth century, yes, but probably not the Oklahoma bombing you're thinking of. Even though Timothy McVeigh's April 19, 1995, bombing that killed 168 people was a terrible act, the dynamite assault on Tulsa's black community in 1921 was worse. A white mob, their simmering prejudice inflamed by a rumor that a black shoe-shiner had assaulted a white woman, began torching Tulsa's 35-block black community (charmingly referred to as Little Africa). Some of the white townspeople, with access to dynamite and an airplane, decided to use both against the black population. The dynamite destroyed at least 1,000 homes; between the bombs, fires, and the mobs, 250 people were killed.

IF I DON'T GET SERVED IN FIVE HOURS, NO TIP!

Where did the first lunch counter sit-in over segregation take place?

At Woolworth's department store in Greensboro, North Carolina. The date was February 1, 1960, and the protest consisted of four black students from North Carolina Agricultural and Technical State University—Franklin McCain, Joseph McNeil, Ezell Blair Jr., and David Richmond—sitting at a "white's only" lunch counter and ordering food and beverages. The sit-in persisted throughout the following days as other young blacks joined them. Simply by waiting patiently for service, the Greensboro sit-ins led to integrated lunch counters at Woolworth's and other department store lunch counters in Greensboro, as well as igniting sit-ins in other cities. It didn't take long before the segregated lunch counter became a thing of the past.

Ask! Is the Montgomery lunch counter, where blacks had their sit-in, still there?

WHITE CANDIDATE SPEAKS WITH FORKED TONGUE

When were Native Americans allowed to vote in U.S. elections?

In 1924, native-born Indians were finally granted American citizenship, and many were allowed to vote at that point. However, in some states they were forbidden from voting until as late as 1954.

ONE WOMAN, ONE VOTE

What modern country was the first to give women the right to vote?

New Zealand in 1893.

What was the first state to give women the vote?

Wyoming, in 1869, when it was still just a territory. Colorado was next in 1893. Utah and Idaho followed in 1896. The next state to grant suffrage was Washington, but it wasn't until after the turn of the century in 1910.

What year was the first woman elected to the U.S. House of Representatives?

1917. Montana had granted women's suffrage in 1914. Three years later, they elected Jeanette Rankin to serve in Congress. She served twice: from 1917 to 1919, and again in 1943.

Rankin is also remembered for being the only congressional vote against American entry into the world wars. In 1941, during the roll call in Congress, she memorably declared: "As a woman, I can't go to war, and I refuse to send anyone else."

Why was the Equal Rights Amendment defeated?

The ERA was an amendment to the United States Constitution that read: "Equality of rights under the law shall not be denied or abridged by the United States or by any state on account of sex." In fact, it was such a commonsensical no-brainer that the U.S. Congress and 35 of the necessary 38 states quickly ratified it in the 1970s. However, that was before certain business interests and religious-right conservatives realized that there could be potential political gain in opposing it. How to oppose equality without looking like fools or bigots was the problem. It required turning the amendment into something it was not. For example, here's Ronald Reagan, candidate for the presidency: "Human beings are not animals, and I do not want to see sex and sexual differences treated as casually and amorally as dogs and other beasts treat them. I believe this could happen under the ERA." Pat Robertson, another presidential wanna-be and television evangelist, declared that the amendment "is about a socialist, anti-family political movement that encourages women to leave their husbands, kill their children, practice witchcraft, destroy capitalism, and become lesbians."

How could you argue against logic like that? Supporters of the Equal Rights Amendment tried to bring the question back to the issue of equality, but their opponents managed to muddy the waters enough so that no additional states supported the ERA. Its ratification deadline expired in 1982, three states short.

WAY DOWN YONDER IN NEW ORLEANS

What's the difference between Creoles and Cajuns?

In 1762, King Louis XV of France gave Louisiana to his cousin, King Charles III of Spain. The new Spanish aristocracy called the French-speaking people who lived there *Criolla,* the Spanish word which means "from this place." Originally, it referred to people of European descent only. Eventually, the original Creoles began using the phrase *negres Creoles* to denote their slaves. (Later, *Creoles de couleur* became used to describe free African Americans who were born in the city.) All of this got more confusing as the tight-knit, French-speaking population interbred across color lines and became neither completely white nor black. This led to a caste system based on who was what percentage of what race. A racial naming system developed that required tracking ancestry back eight generations and totaling the racial makeup of each of your 128 great-great-great-great-great-great grandparents. No, we're not kidding.

If all 128 of these ancestors were white, you were considered white. However, if even *one* of them was non-white, you were considered non-white. Within that designation was an even more absurd series of graduated distinctions. For example, if 127 of your ancestors were white, you were considered *sang melee*. If 120, *mamelouque*. If 112, *octoroon*. If 96, *quadroon*. If 64, *mulatto*. And so on, all the way to *negro* for those who had zero white ancestors.

Luckily, Cajuns are much easier. Because they were considered white-trash newcomers, there were no caste distinctions made about them. In fact, many were forced into the swamps and backcountry as the Creoles took over their land during an economic downturn in the late 1800s.

Where did Cajuns come from, and where'd they get the name? The answer to both lies thousands of miles northeast in Acadia, a French colony founded by about 100 families near Canada's Bay of Fundy in 1604. During the French and Indian War in 1755, British troops drove the French Acadians from their homes. Of the 10,000 refugees, about 4,000 of them decided to relocate to French-speaking New Orleans, where they hoped they'd get a warm *bon jour* from the Creoles. No such luck. For one thing, the Creoles fancied themselves French aristocrats. They didn't cotton much to the Acadians, who were more democratic and plebian and less interested in creating fiefdoms than small ranches and farms. The Acadians, or Cajuns as they came to be called by Americans, became marginalized. The hardships they suffered as tenant farmers led to another migration by many of them from Louisiana to Texas refineries and shipyards early in the 20th century. Those who stayed, mostly in poverty, found their language and culture besieged (for example, the state of Louisiana passed anti-Cajun laws, including one that forbid using Cajun French in public schools in 1921).

Finally, in the 1960s, when other groups began to assert ethnic pride, young college-educated Cajuns began to do the same. In 1968, public pressure pushed the Louisiana state legislature to establish a council to reverse the decline of Cajun culture. A renaissance of spicy Cajun cooking and good ol' swamp music brought this little-known group to the attention of the nation, and probably made those dastardly Canadians feel a little sorry that they'd sent them away.

APPOINTMENT AND DISAPPOINTMENT

How many African Americans have served on the Supreme Court?

Only two. The first, Thurgood Marshall, was a widely recognized civil rights theorist who had headed the NAACP. He had been an accomplished attorney who convinced the 1954 Supreme Court that racial segregation in public schools was unconstitutional, and he was a respected jurist with years of experience on the federal bench. The second African American to serve on the Supreme Court was Clarence Thomas.

DIVISIONS OF RACE AND CLASS

Who was "Brown" in the case of Brown vs. the Board of Education?

His name was Oliver Brown, and he was a boxcar welder for the railroad in Topeka, Kansas. He sued the Topeka Board of Education because his young daughter Linda couldn't attend the all-white Sumner Elementary School near his home. Brown ultimately won this civil rights legal battle before the Supreme Court. Lawyer Thurgood Marshall successfully argued that segregation violated the 14th Amendment ("Section 1. All persons born or naturalized in the United States, and subject to the jurisdiction thereof, are citizens of the United States and of the state wherein they reside. No state shall make or enforce any law which shall abridge the privileges or immunities of citizens of the United States; nor shall any state deprive any person of life, liberty, or property, without due process of law; nor deny to any person within its jurisdiction the equal protection of the laws."). Regardless, it still took years and many fights before all public schools in the U.S. obeyed the law. Particularly slow in adhering were public schools in the southern United States.

GOT MLK?

Where did Martin Luther King Jr. give his "I Have a Dream" speech?

In front of the Lincoln Memorial in Washington, D.C., during the 1963 March on Washington.

How many heard Martin Luther King Jr. give his "I Have a Dream" speech live?

Despite the worries of the organizers that no one would attend out of fear of being assaulted and arrested by police or angry mobs, well over 200,000 peaceful protesters showed up that day. An *L.A. Times* reporter memorably wrote in his coverage of the event: "No one could ever remember an invading army quite as gentle as the two hundred thousand civil rights marchers who occupied Washington."

Ask! Can I see or hear Martin Luther King's "I Have a Dream" speech online?

Did Martin Luther King Jr. and Malcolm X work together on civil rights issues?

No, not together. As a matter of fact, they were critical of each other's methods of fighting for equality. Malcolm X believed that equal rights for blacks should be had "by any means necessary," up to and including war and death. Dr. Martin Luther King Jr. believed in a completely nonviolent approach. They did meet once, during the U.S. Senate debate over the Civil Rights Bill in 1964, and although their opinions about civil rights issues grew closer toward the end of Malcolm X's life, their philosophies on methods of achieving this equality were always at odds.

What was Dr. Martin Luther King Jr. a doctor of?

He had a doctorate degree in theology from Crozer Theological Seminary in Pennsylvania.

THE X FILES

What was Malcolm X's real name?

He was born Malcolm Little to Earl and Louise Little in Omaha, Nebraska, in 1925. He chose the "X" to represent the unknown names of his African ancestors.

Besides Roots, *what else did author Alex Haley write?*

The Autobiography of Malcolm X in 1965, for one. Malcolm X never saw the book. He was killed right before the manuscript went to press. Other literary works by Haley include a biography of the security guard Frank Wills (who discovered the break-in at Watergate), *A Different Kind of Christmas,* and his last book, *Queen,* in 1993 (completed by David Stevens). Haley died in early 1992.

THE BRITISH ISLES

From a Scotsman's kilt to Londonderry Air, the British Isles have stood the test of time and continue to capture the romantic imaginations of the entire world. Here are some of the more interesting questions asked of Jeeves about his homeland.

SEEMS LIKE OLD THAMES

How old is London's Tower Bridge?

First of all, many tourists assume that the Tower Bridge is really the more famous (but less impressive) London Bridge. Even those who know its real name assume that it is about as old as its ancient neighbor, the Tower of London. But it was finished in 1894, making it younger than even the Brooklyn Bridge.

Who's the "Ben" responsible for the name of the Big Ben clock?

The name Big Ben doesn't refer to the chapel clock, but to the 13-ton bell that rings in the clock tower. The "Ben" behind the bell was Sir Benjamin Hall, the first commissioner of works at the time of installation in 1856. A loud man, it's said. So the name was very appropriate.

During business trips to London I've noticed that the light above the clock face of Big Ben is sometimes lit and sometimes not. Any rhyme or reason to this?

You're an observant sort. There is a traditional reason, actually: When the light is shining, Parliament is in session. We guess the lords wanted to be able to keep track of the time.

Who was "the Iron Lady"?

The 1980s British leader Margaret Thatcher. "The Iron Lady" was a nickname given by a Russian newspaper, and the name stuck. Not to be confused with "Iron Maiden," which was the name of both a medieval execution device and a torturous 1970s rock band.

Who came up with the term "Iron Curtain"?

The easy answer is Winston Churchill. In most history texts, you'll find that he used the term publicly in a speech given at Westminster College in Fulton, Missouri, in 1946. Jeeves's handy little *Oxford Dictionary of Quotations,* however, says the term was in use long before his speech. "The expression 'iron curtain' had been previously applied by others to the Soviet Union or its sphere of influence, e.g., Ethel Snowden, *Through Bolshevik Russia* (1920); Dr. Goebbels, *Das Reich* (25 Feb. 1945); and by Churchill himself in a cable to President Truman (4 June 1945)." Because Churchill's speech was widely heard (and heard of), people assumed that he actually coined the phrase; however, he didn't.

I know he was photographed with cigars, but how much did the British prime minister, Winston Churchill, really smoke?

They weren't just photo props. It's estimated that Churchill smoked 300,000 cigars in his lifetime.

Is it true that Winston Churchill suffered terribly from depression?

It's true. Churchill suffered from what was then called *melancholia* and what we now call depression. He referred to it as "the black dog," and the only thing that seemed to relieve it, to his horror, was aggression. He took up bullying at a young age and seemed to get a certain amount of pleasure from it. Political duties, if they happened to involve conflict or bloodshed, seemed to also bring a certain satisfaction to Churchill. Once he sent the army to squelch a miners' strike by force. In a confession, of sorts, he said at the time, "Everything is gearing towards catastrophe and collapse. I am interested, geared up, and happy. Is it not horrible to be built like this?"

Depression ran heavily in Churchill's family for at least five generations. His father, a depression sufferer himself, had the added burden of insanity, produced by the middle and late stages of syphilis. The depression bug carried over to Churchill's four children, only one of whom seemed to lead a relatively peaceful and happy life. His son, Randolph, and his daughter, Sarah, battled alcoholism and depression all of their lives, and his daughter Diana killed herself. Churchill also had a niece who attempted suicide, only to be left brain-damaged and still depressed.

Is it any wonder, then, that the family motto was *Fiel pero desdichado,* "Faithful but unfortunate"?

Ask! Where can I see pictures of Stonehenge?

UP IN SMOKE

Is London's famous fog natural or air pollution?

Air pollution. It's been a problem in London for almost 1,000 years, beginning at a time in history when wood supplies started running out. The people of the city began using sea coal for heat and cooking, which wasn't very efficient and produced an abundance of smoke in the air. At one point, the pollution got so ghastly that torture and death was the sentence for anyone caught using coal, but wood prices were so high it was an impossible law for the crown to enforce.

The "fog" was so bad during Shakespearean times that it made its way into *MacBeth*. Remember the witches' chant? "Fair is foul, and foul is fair: Hover through the fog and filthy air."

Things got worse in the 1950s when London scrapped its electric tram system for diesel bus lines. That one simple act added huge amounts of pollution to the smoke-filled London air, and the results were devastating. As many as 4,000 people died of pollution-related causes in December 1952. The number of deaths per day in London rose from 135 to more than 500 a day and stayed above the 200 mark for three weeks. At the time, despite the alarming jump in death rates, the government refused to acknowledge the issue. (For that matter, death certificates don't usually say "cause of death: smog.") In 1956, Parliament caved to scientific evidence and public outcry and passed the Clean Air Act, which created "smokeless zones"—areas that could only burn smokeless fuels—and relocated power stations to more remote areas outside of London.

What are the origins of the word "smog"?

It was originally coined by a French scientist, Dr. Des Voeux, at a July 3, 1905, Public Health Council meeting in London as a description for its worrisome pollution-saturated fog. The word was created by blending the words "smoke" and "fog."

THE FAWKES & THE HOUNDS

What's the English celebration called Bonfire Night about?

Bonfire Night is another name for Guy Fawkes Day, a uniquely British holiday. Celebrations are held in every town and neighborhood, with huge bonfires, children in masks, firecrackers, and burning effigies of Guy Fawkes—the 17th-century traitor who, along with his band of coconspirators, tried to blow up the Parliament building as a protest to the way the British government was treating Catholics in the kingdom.

As the story goes (and there are those who argue that many of the facts were rearranged by the final victors, the English government), the group managed to actually sneak kegs of gun powder below the Parliament building. Before they could set it off, however, some of them got cold feet and one of them snitched. On November 5, 1605, Guy Fawkes was found and arrested in a cellar below Parliament, standing alongside 36 barrels of gun powder and said to be waiting to light the fuse.

The people of England, upon hearing that their king, James I, had been saved from the terrorist attack, lit bonfires in thanksgiving. On that date ever since, bonfires are lit in every corner of England, and straw effigies of Guy Fawkes and sometimes the pope are then tossed into the fire to burn (in past centuries, this ceremony was often accompanied by an anti-Catholic homily). Finally, firecrackers are set off in remembrance of the big bang that could've toppled their Anglican government.

NAKED AMBITION

Did Lady Godiva really exist?

Because so many of the great British legends have been proven to be patently untrue, many people assume that the Lady Godiva story is equally false. Yet according to accounts by 13th- and 14th-century historians, the core of the story is true.

Here's what they report: Godiva (also sometimes spelled *Godgifu*) was the wife of Leofric, Earl of Mercia. Leofric had made his fortune in the mutton trade in the working-class town of Shrewsbury, and in about 1040 A.D., the socially ambitious couple decided to move on up to a better town. They chose Coventry in Warwickshire. As newcomers and members of the nouveau riche, Godiva and Leofric worked hard to make their mark on local society. Godiva became a patron of the arts and her husband became active in the church and local government, where he quickly climbed into a position of power.

Leofric began an ambitious program of public works projects, including a new waterworks and church. To pay for them, he began levying taxes wherever he could, which included a widely unpopular tax on manure. Godiva, wanting to elevate the aesthetic and spiritual lives of the peasants, discovered that her work was being thwarted by the new taxes. The peasants suddenly didn't have much energy left for spirituality and art appreciation when they were having trouble feeding, clothing, and sheltering themselves. Furthermore, the fact that it was her own husband who was adding to their troubles didn't increase their affection toward the lady, no matter how good-hearted she may have been.

Godiva reportedly confronted her husband during a meeting of the village councilmen. He responded with incredulousness: scale back his important works so that the peasants can learn about "the finer things in life"? He literally fell off his stool chuckling at the ideas of this endearingly impractical young woman he'd married, spraining his wrist in the process. He dismissed her with the comment that perhaps he should add a tax on all new art, since she'd probably be the only one who would have to pay it.

Godiva didn't give up, and Leofric wouldn't give in. After weeks of matrimonial feuding, he finally came up with the sporting proposition that we all know of: He'd drop all the taxes he'd added if she'd ride through the marketplace at its noon peak, stark naked. After all, he added, if she believed that the human body was beautiful in art, wouldn't seeing her beautiful, unclothed body have an elevating effect on the peasants and bring them to a greater appreciation of beauty? Godiva considered the proposition, asked for her husband's permission to do as he suggested, and then, to his shock, agreed to his terms.

Historians establish that the ride took place in 1056 A.D. They tell us that Godiva rode at noon as instructed, accompanied by two clothed female aides on horses. Her hair was braided and curled snugly against the back of her head, and she wore no jewelry or other adornments. News of the event had circulated throughout the town; in anticipation, the market was filled with curious onlookers. They were impressed with her relaxed, confident, and unashamed manner, writes writer and historian Jerome Krause, perhaps unintentionally adding still another level of mythology: "To all present this was an experience like no other in their lives. . . . She was not merely naked; rather she was in a higher state of presentation . . . beyond voyeurism." And the historical accounts indicate that, true to his word, her husband, Leofric, scaled back his plans and brought taxes down to the level where they had been when he first took office.

Hey, what about the other parts of the Lady Goldiva story—her long hair, Peeping Tom, etc.?

All embellishments of prudish churchmen in the 17th century. You know the elements: At noon on the appointed day, the streets were completely cleared of people; Godiva's freakishly long hair hid all the good parts anyway; and a "Peeping Tom" looked out his window and was immediately blinded. According to historians, these aspects of the classic story are all lies.

ERRIN' FACTS

How old is the tradition of serving corned beef and cabbage on St. Patrick's Day?

Only about a hundred years old, and it didn't actually originate in Ireland. It came from ye old Emerald Island—Manhattan in New York City—at the beginning of the 20th century, when Irish immigrants to New York's Lower East Side adopted corned beef from their Jewish neighbors.

Another tradition that came from the New World, not Ireland, is the drunken revelry of the St. Patrick's Day parade. Back in Ireland, St. Patrick's Day had been a religious holiday meant for quiet reflection and church (in fact, pubs in Ireland were closed on St. Patrick's Day until the 1970s), but Irish Americans decided it was an occasion to show off their numbers and political clout by marching through big cities. Eventually, the Ireland Irish followed suit.

Still another Irish tradition that came from America, not Ireland, is that of the friendly, mischievous leprechaun. Even though the legend of leprechauns existed back in Ireland, the little green guys were a nasty race you wouldn't want to meet up with. But Disney and Lucky Charms cereal helped put an end to that image.

Did St. Patrick really drive the snakes from Ireland?

No, there never were any native snakes in Ireland. Also, despite legend, he didn't use the shamrock to illustrate the Christian doctrine of the three-Gods-in-one trinity. The first written mention of this idea didn't appear until ten centuries after Patrick's death.

What's the story behind the Blarney Stone?

The Blarney Stone is so named because it resides at the top of Blarney Castle just outside the town of Blarney. It's at least the third castle that's been built on the same spot, this one in the 15th century by the Lord of Blarney, Cormac Laidhiv McCathy.

McCathy, like all Irish lords at the time, was in a pinch with the British Queen Elizabeth I. As if it weren't enough that he was battling Cromwellians and William III's troops around his castle by day, he was also battling the British crown—if not with weapons, then with words—to keep control over his land and home. A representative of the queen would come by, and McCathy would agree to turn over land owed to the crown. Time after time, these promises were never made good on, and the representative returned to the queen with news that she didn't yet have the Blarney Castle. As the story goes, this happened so many times that Queen Elizabeth began to roll her eyes and say, "no more Blarney talk!"

Legends grew from the stone and the newfound meaning of the word blarney (now meaning "persuasive eloquence"). Many revolve around an old woman casting a spell on the stone after the king of the region saved her from drowning. The spell would forever give him the "gift of gab." For over 500 years, visitors have hung upside down and backward to plant their lips on the stone at the top of the castle, hoping to suddenly be able to talk their way out of anything. Ironically, *blarney* (or *an blarna)* in Gaelic means "the plain."

Ask!

Can I virtually kiss the Blarney Stone?

Were the British conquerors at least fans of Irish music?

No. They considered Celtic music to be a destabilizing force, galvanizing resistance, stirring up emotions, and reminding the Irish of their pre-occupation history. They outlawed it, and Queen Elizabeth I decreed that musicians were to be arrested and hanged on the spot. This severe repression of Irish culture lasted for over 100 years.

When did Chicago start dyeing its river green on St. Patrick's Day?

1962. It's vegetable dye, believed to be harmless.

IT'S ALL GREEK TO ME

Do Scottish, Irish, and Welsh people all speak the same language?

The history of the Gaelic languages is complicated, beginning over 2,500 years ago, and it involves many conquerings and several migrations. Originally, they spoke the same language and came from the same people—the Celts. The Celts eventually broke off into various groups all over Europe, ranging from the Iberian Peninsula (Spain and Portugal) to Gaul (France). This latter group migrated a tad north, becoming the Irish and Scottish Gaelics ("Galtae"). Unfortunately, because of these new cultural separations, the Roman Empire was able to overthrow much of formerly Celtic Europe.

However, Ireland, being isolated by water and distance, managed to maintain its heritage as the Romans conquered the rest of the continent. The people, known as the Gaels, migrated north into modern day Scotland. The Romans called them "Scottis," giving them their current name. Even though the British eventually took Scotland, the Scottish were able to maintain their distinct culture and language over the years. Despite the variations in culture and speech that ensued, the two Gaelics, Irish and Scottish, are quite similar.

Welsh, on the other hand, although coming from very similar origins, looks and sounds like a foreign language by comparison. The Welsh, Cornish, Breton, and Cumbric languages all stem from the Scottish/Irish Celtic language, but due to its isolation, it also morphed into something totally unique. Their brand of Celtic is called Brythonic, and it's particular to the west coast of Britain.

Ask!
Where can I find an online Gaelic primer?

What's the difference between Mc and Mac?

Forget everything you know: "Mc" isn't the Irish equivalent to the Scottish "Mac," nor does the difference denote socioeconomic status. "Mc" is simply an abbreviation of "Mac." Any amateur genealogist has learned to be phonetically tolerant in the search for last names, and the Mac bunch is no exception.

Incidentally, "Mac" is the Gaelic word for "son." Hence, MacDonald (or McDonald) is literally "son of Donald"; meaning exactly the same as the last name Donaldson.

AM I BLUE?

Did the real "Braveheart" paint his face blue before battle?

No, William Wallace didn't paint himself or his comrades before going into battle. This was the stuff of Hollywood screenwriter Randall Wallace (no relation) and his director sidekick, Mel Gibson. It proved a good theatrical addition, and didn't substantially change the real story of the Scottish hero. The same can't be said for other changes Mel and his folks made. See what you think. Other historical inaccuracies in the movie include:

- ◆ **The death of Wallace's father:** William was probably more like 20 instead of 8.

- ◆ **Princess Isabella as lover:** That this happened is highly doubtful. She would've been a mere child at the time. Most important, she wouldn't have been sent on diplomatic trips for her father, the King of France, whatever her age.

- ◆ **English soldiers and the rape of Scottish brides:** However nasty English soldiers were to Scottish women (and they were nasty), there's no indication that a systematic raping of Scottish women on their wedding nights was ever in place or that it was ordered by Edward I's throne.

- ◆ **Bare-bottoming the Brits:** Exposing their bums to English soldiers was not the reason they won the battle of Stiling Bridge.

THE SECRETS OF A GOOD SCOTCH

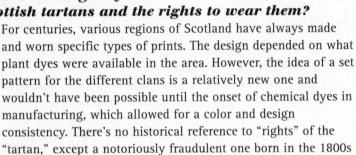

Where can I see a picture of what's under a kilt? **Ask!**

What did Scottish guys wear under their kilts?

Traditionally, not a thing.

What's the origin of the Scottish tartans and the rights to wear them?

For centuries, various regions of Scotland have always made and worn specific types of prints. The design depended on what plant dyes were available in the area. However, the idea of a set pattern for the different clans is a relatively new one and wouldn't have been possible until the onset of chemical dyes in manufacturing, which allowed for a color and design consistency. There's no historical reference to "rights" of the "tartan," except a notoriously fraudulent one born in the 1800s that became legend.

The Scottish scene in the early 1800s was this: The wealthy landowners ("chiefs") decided they could earn more money if they kicked the common people off their land and brought in sheep. Class division was never greater than at this time of Scottish dispersion.

Then in walks an unlikely pair who took note of the consumer needs of the gentry: two Polish brothers claiming to be the grandsons of Bonnie Prince Charlie, who called themselves the Sobieski Stolberg Stuarts. The swindler brothers decided to market a book about the sovereignty of the Scottish clans and their chiefs. This book, titled *Vestiarium Scoticum* claimed to have access to a 16th-century manuscript that detailed all of the tartans and which clans they belonged to. The wealthy snatched up the brothers' book, eager to identify their own clan and legitimize the land they'd gobbled up from the Scottish people. Aiding in the spreading of the word were the likes of Scottish enthusiasts Queen Victoria and Prince Albert, along with Sir

Walter Raleigh and others, who wrote of these supposed ancient traditions and rights.

By the time the Stolberg Stuarts and their claims were proven complete frauds, the idea had become ingrained in the minds of the world.

What clan was the classic Aladdin plaid lunchbox and thermos from?

Laddie, the lunch pail, by all our powers o' kenning, looks to be related to the Wemyss clan.

Ask! Is there a Scottish tartan online database?

HISTORICAL
HODGEPODGE

Rather than willy-nilly discarding the short odds and sods that didn't fit neatly into the nooks and crannies of this book, Jeeves has decided to toss them higgledy-piggledy into this hodgepodge of a chapter.

OUT OF AFRICA

How long was Nelson Mandela in prison before becoming prime minister of South Africa?

Twenty-eight years.

When and where was steel first produced?

By all indications, in eastern Africa sometime around 1400 B.C. The technology spread slowly; it wasn't until the first century A.D. that the rest of the continent was also producing steel. Africans were first elsewhere, too: Even the Iron Age had come early to the continent, probably in the sixth century B.C.

Who was known as "the African Emperor"?

The first of the African Roman emperors, Septimius Severus, ruled from 193 to 211 A.D. He was born in April of 146 in the ancient city of Lepcis Magna (modern day Libya), which was, at the time, part of the Roman Empire. His family had become Roman citizens when he was young, and Severus decided to pursue a military career within the Roman ranks. Slowly, he gained power, taking the throne as he neared 50 years old. Severus had a bloody but just reign over the Roman Empire, constantly battling to preserve Roman borders and squelching political rivals. He died at York in 211 while strengthening Roman rule in Britain, leaving his sons the empire.

What does "tsetse" mean in African?

Besides being the name of a blood-sucking fly that spreads African sleeping sickness, it's also a Bantu people's name for the lightning character in an African creation story. Is there a connection between the two? Nobody seems to know.

LOOK LUCY, HE HAS A LEAKY SKULL

Where did they get the name Homo erectus, and can paleontologists say the name without snickering?

Well, all we know is that we here at the "Ask Jeeves" book desk giggle like school kids whenever we have occasion to say *"Homo erectus."* Even knowing that it means "upright man" doesn't dampen our exuberant mirth. In fact, it only seems to add to it. But we don't get out much, and we aren't paleontologists, so we suspect they're a little more serious than we are.

Homo erectus got his name, of course, for walking straighter than some of his earlier ancestors. He could've also been called something else, since other early-human names are more descriptive of their accomplishments than their physical characteristics (like his early work with taming fire, perhaps). For example, *Homo habitus,* which means "handy man," in honor of their being the first to make stone tools. Or *Homo sapiens,* which means—despite the overwhelming evidence around you proving otherwise—"wise man." Now if *that* doesn't get paleontologists snickering, what will?

Did Neanderthals leave any art?

No. Even though they did have brains as large as ours and lived concurrently with *Homo sapiens* at a time when humans were making tools, painting caves, and traveling the sea, the Neanderthals were apparently a pretty dim cousin; hence the derogatory term. There's no known art from them, and no evidence of technological advancement, leaving a strong suspicion that these strong silent types were literally that. They may have never even developed a language. The Neanderthals died out about 35,000 years ago; *Homo sapiens* aren't due to go extinct for at least another decade or two.

Ask!
Where can I see Ice Age art?

OVER BERING STRAIT

Was England ever connected to Europe?

Yes, and not that long ago. Early humans walked over the land bridge to England about 500,000 years ago and stayed there— despite the depressing winters!—even as the waters rose and made escape to the Riviera impossible.

WWJBD (WHAT WOULD JAMES BOND DO)?

Did the United States government plan to kill Fidel Castro? How?

We may never know all of the ways, but from the ones we do know of, you can certainly see the effect that reading too many James Bond novels had on John Kennedy and his staff. Here are some of the wilder plots:

- Inject botulism toxin into Castro's favorite brand of cigars and give him a gift box
- Dissolve botulism into a drink for Castro
- Infect scuba equipment with deadly germs and present it to avid scuba diver Castro as a gift
- Booby-trap a seashell to explode if removed from the ocean floor by Castro
- Equip a fountain pen with a hidden needle for injecting a lethal toxin and ask Castro for an autograph
- Shoot him with high-powered rifles with telescopic sights—presumably from a book depository building and a grassy knoll

Even after somebody actually used the last one on Kennedy himself—quite possibly Lee Harvey Oswald, who had read pro-Cuban magazines that detailed some of the assassination attempts against Castro—the plotting against Castro continued.

What were Operation Dirty Trick and Operation Bingo?

Early 1960s American schemes to create a politically defensible excuse for invading Cuba. Operation Bingo was a plan to fake an attack on the United States Guantánamo Bay military base as a pretext for a devastating U.S. military assault on Havana. Operation Dirty Trick was a plan to kill two birds with one stone if something went wrong with the manned 1962 Mercury space flight, carrying John Glenn: Forged documentation and doctored photos were readied in order to blame any mission disaster not on NASA but on the Cuban government. These were just two of many plots dreamed up for Operation Moongoose, a secret program created by Robert Kennedy during his brother's administration. Details were revealed in documents declassified in 1997.

I SPY

Where did Julia Child train as a chef?

When she was 37 years old, she enrolled in the famous Cordon Bleu cooking school in Paris. Before that, she took hints from the classic *The Joy of Cooking* and experimented often on her new husband and their friends. Before that, you ask? Before that, Julia McWilliams (she hadn't yet married Paul Child) served in what was the precursor to the CIA in Ceylon (Sri Lanka) and China—the Office of Strategic Services. That's right, TVs best-known food maven was a spy!

What was the real name and nationality of Mata Hari?

Mata Hari was executed by a French firing squad for being a German spy during World War I. She had been popular in Europe as a "Javanese" dancer but was really Dutch, born with the somewhat less exotic name Margaretha Geertruida Zelle. Mata Hari was her stage name.

TURN ON, TUNE IN, BETRAY YOUR COUNTRY

I've heard the name but don't know who Tokyo Rose really was. A spy?

During World War II, "Tokyo Rose" was the nickname for several Japanese deejays who broadcast propaganda to American sailors in the Pacific. The most notorious one was Iva Ikuko Toguri (aka, "Orphan Ann") a Japanese American born and raised in Los Angeles. She became stranded in Japan after visiting relatives there prior to the Japanese attack on Pearl Harbor and tried to make the most of a bad situation. Tried and convicted in the U.S. after the war, she was pardoned by President Ford in 1974.

Other notorious World War II propagandists were the American "Axis Sally" (Mildred Gillars), and the American-born/British-raised Lord Haw Haw (William Joyce)—both deejays broadcasting for the Germans to British and American soldiers fighting in Europe.

Ask! Can I hear broadcasts by Tokyo Rose on the Internet?

THE FALCON FLIES AT MIDNIGHT

Why did the English spy agency raise falcons during World War II?

They had discovered that German spies were using pigeons to send messages to bases over the English Channel. S.S. leader Heinrich Himmler was a pigeon fancier (and in fact was the president of the German National Pigeon Society). The Nazis confiscated pigeons from their owners to use for the war effort, and baskets of pigeons were smuggled into England by human smugglers, submarines, and parachutists.

To counter the menace, the MI5 spy agency tamed and trained its own crack force of peregrine falcons. They patrolled the air over the British coasts in two-hour shifts, and took down any pigeons flying off toward the mainland.

BAD MEDICINE

When did people figure out that smoking was bad for you?

It's a common myth that the hazards of smoking weren't known until sometime in this century. Almost as long as tobacco has inhabited western civilization, most have been aware of its serious ill effects.

Explorer Rodrigo de Jerez was probably the first European to take up smoking, sometime around 1492 when he accompanied Columbus on his journey to the New World. As the practice spread, a slew of governments and the Roman Catholic Church outlawed the practice, in part for moral reasons and in part because it smelled bad, looked scary, and made you cough. By the early 1600s, many were drawing the correlation between illnesses suffered by chimney sweeps and those that showed up in smokers. In 1604, King James published his edict against smoking, *A Counterblaste to Tobacco,* which included notes from autopsies of smokers. Their "inward parts," it read, were "infected with an oily kind of soot." But King James also realized that to ban tobacco use meant his government would lose tobacco tax revenues. Thus began a tradition of governments sugar-coating fact to maintain income from the sale of tobacco.

In 1761, Dr. John Hill performed clinical studies showing a direct correlation between snuff use and nose cancer. In the same year, Dr. Percival Pott studied chimney sweeps and found a direct connection between soot and cancer of the scrotum. Over time, researchers linked more and more illnesses to smoking. The evidence was so overwhelming by the 1950s that tobacco companies introduced filtered cigarettes in the hope that consumers might be fooled into thinking they were safer. Finally, the government issued a report in 1964 that pretty much confirmed what King James knew in 1604: That smoking is "Lothesome to the eye, hatefull to the Nose, harmfull to the braine, dangerous to the Lungs, and in the stinking fume thereof, nearest resembling the horrific Stigian smoke of the pit that is bottomless."

Why was bloodletting thought to heal the sick?

Long after the rest of the world—the Ottomans, the Chinese, the Byzantines—had realized the finer points of anatomy and physiology, western Europe stayed stuck in an old paradigm they'd learned from the ancient Greeks. It went something like this: The body consisted of the four humours (fluids): blood, yellow bile, phlegm, and black bile. In order for the body, mind, and character to be healthy, these four fluids needed to be in perfect balance. If something were wrong in the body or mind, something must be wrong with the humours.

The diagnosis? If someone were lecherous, warlike, and rash, they had a hefty presence of blood. If angry, violent, or vengeful, that could be attributed to an excess of yellow bile. Cowardice, paleness, or dullness could be blamed on too much phlegm, and too much black bile was indicated by laziness, an overwrought disposition, or gluttony.

Common medical belief held that a good diet, exercise, and a good environment would keep the four humours in balance. If they got out of wack, there were plenty of noninvasive remedies: laxatives or diuretics, hot baths with herbs, smoke from burning herbs, or in the case of injury, cauterization and sterilization of the wound.

For more serious situations, bloodletting was used. The reasoning behind the procedure was that if blood amounts were lowered, the other fluids would fall into balance. It was a crazy idea, and it didn't work. Bloodletting killed more people than it cured, yet it was performed on the sick well into the 19th century.

GIVE 'EM AN INCH

Why is the mile 5,280 feet instead of an even 5,000 or something?

Blame it on the Tudors and their fondness for the furlong. Originally, the mile was 5,000 feet, but Elizabeth I decided that the mile should be divisible by an equal number of furlongs (one furlong measures exactly 220 yards, or 660 feet). In 1575 she passed a law adding 280 more feet to the official mile so that it equaled eight furlongs.

Why is a marathon 26.2 miles instead of exactly 26?

This is yet another distance forever changed by the British royalty. The marathon used to be less than 26 miles. For the modern Olympics in 1896, the marathon distance was determined by the distance from Marathon Bridge, where the race began, to the Olympic stadium in Athens—24.85 miles, or an even 40 kilometers. In 1908, the distance was lengthened to an even 26 miles as it ran between Windsor Castle and White City stadium. But another 385 yards were tacked on to the end so that the race could finish right in front of the royal family's viewing box. For some reason, the 1908 distance stuck. In 1921 the International Amateur Athletic Foundation (IAAF) officially adopted the 1908 distance of 26 miles, 385 yards (26.2 miles or 42 kilometers) as the marathon distance.

What exactly is a "fathom" and why didn't sailors just use feet?

A fathom is now considered exactly six feet, but it wasn't always quite so standardized. In the days of the Vikings, they measured one fathom by extending their arms as far as they could reach; *"fathom"* in old Norse means "embrace."

Did "rule of thumb" come from English Common Law, dictating that men could beat their wives as long as they used a stick no bigger than a thumb's width?

No. Although the myth has been cluelessly cited as fact over and over again in news articles and in other media outlets, there was no such English Common Law. There was no such law anywhere in the United States, either, and wife-beating was officially against the law in the American colonies long before the Revolution. The expression "rule of thumb" is derived from the carpentry profession; essentially as a way of estimating an inch.

DOLLARS AND SENSE

Where did the dollar symbol come from? What does "$" mean?

It's a good question without a definitive answer. However, there is a likely explanation that is (reluctantly) accepted, in lieu of any exact proof of origin. In early America, various currency was used: French, English, Italian, and Spanish—whatever coins were available. The Spanish *peso* was most frequently traded, and it became common to write the abbreviation for *pesos*—*ps*—instead of writing out the whole word, as in *ps 12* instead of *12 pesos*. From there, *ps* was intertwined even more (a shorthand version, as it were) with the *p* and the *s* overlapping. The *p*'s front part sort of disappeared as an unnecessary stroke, and we're left with the dollar sign we use today.

When was the first time in history a company made a billion dollars in one year?

It was General Motors, back in 1955.

Who's Carnegie, and why are so many libraries named after him?

Andrew Carnegie made his millions in Pittsburgh steel. He then sold his company to J. P. Morgan in 1901 and became the richest man in the world with over $500 million dollars (about $10.3 billion in today's money). When he retired, Carnegie put all of his energy into writing essays and books devoted to the question of how to improve society. He was a great believer in education and resources, and he put his money where his mouth was, giving $350 million to various causes and funds. His first public gift was donating baths to his hometown of Dunfermline, Scotland, in 1873. After that he decided to give money to help cities all over the world build libraries. In all, 2,500 libraries were built; 1,700 in the U.S.

His generosity continued. Carnegie financed construction of Carnegie Hall in New York City. He began technical schools in Pittsburgh, which formed the core of Carnegie Mellon University. The Carnegie Institute in Washington, D.C., encourages scientific research. He was a benefactor of the African American Tuskegee Institute as well. There are Carnegie funds that reward acts of bravery, works to end war, and research into education and public affairs. The Carnegie Foundation for the Advancement of Teaching provides pensions for college professors, and until the government kicked in pensions for presidential widows, Andrew Carnegie's wealth also supported these former first ladies.

His philosophy was strong: At the age of 33, when he began to earn $50,000 a year, he decided that was enough money for anyone for a year's work. He said, "Beyond this never earn, make no effort to increase fortune, but spend the surplus each year for benevolent purposes." If only there were more CEOs like him in our time.

ORIGIN OF A NAME

Why did scientist Carl Sagan sue Apple Computers?

It has been a long-standing practice at Apple to name their in-house, test-model computers after much-respected people. However, when Carl Sagan first got whiff that the company was calling their pre-released Power Mac 7100 the "Sagan," he was less than flattered. He complained, and the company changed the name of the in-house computer to "BHA." Upon learning that BHA stood for "Butthead Astronomer," Sagan took Apple to court. In 1994, Apple won the first round of litigation, then during an appeal settled for an undisclosed amount with the disgruntled scientist.

Where did that '80s group REO Speedwagon get its name?

It was the name of an early 1900s flatbed truck, put out by the REO Motor Vehicle Company. The company was named after its founder, Ransom Eli Olds. After Ransom Olds sold his Oldsmobile Company in 1904, he couldn't legally use his name again for a second company, and opted for his initials instead: R.E.O. Because they were fast and able to carry equipment, many fire departments found the REO Speedwagon especially useful as fire trucks and adapted them as such. The name of this antique truck sounded cool to the band, and so they adopted it and decided to "take it on the run, baby."

All good things must come to an end: childhood, life, love, this book. In this spirit, we bring you some tragi-comic endings from history.

DYING IS EASY, COMEDY IS HARD

Who was it who died because a turtle landed on his head?

According to legend, Greek playwright Aeschylus met his death when a hungry eagle mistook his bald head for a rock and dropped a tortoise on it. Hey, sounds plausible to us, especially when you consider some of the other ways famous people in history have died:

- Curiosity, plain and simple, killed Pliny the Elder. According to his nephew, Pliny the Younger, the Elder began sailing toward Pompeii as Mount Vesuvius was erupting. He was showered with stones from the eruption, but still he sailed onward, wanting a closer look. He landed and camped out the night. The next morning, as ash and smoke engulfed his camp, his crew members fled, but Pliny the Elder stayed and was asphyxiated.

- Saint Lawrence was tied to a barbeque spit and slow-roasted alive by the Roman government. During the ordeal, he was quoted as announcing, "Turn me. I am roasted on one side." When the story spread, Lawrence's humor in the face of death was the catalyst for thousands of conversions and part of what landed him his sainthood.

- In 1216, when King John suffered a bout of blues from losing a fortune, he stopped caring much about his diet, absentmindedly chowing on unripened peaches and cider. In the end, the lousy diet of too much fruit and ale brought on a bad case of diarrhea that took his life. This made for a lousy ending, so when Shakespeare wrote the play *King John,* he opted to off the king with a dose of toad poison instead.

- Danish astronomer Tycho Brahe, otherwise known to be an arrogant sort, surprisingly died from being polite. While at a formal dinner in 1601, he found himself needing to urinate badly. Considering it rude to excuse himself during dinner, Brahe remained seated throughout until his bladder literally burst, killing him.

- During Louis XIV's reign, the famous composer/conductor Jean Baptiste Lully used a baton that was more like a large staff, which he beat upon the floor to keep the musicians in tempo. During one fateful performance in 1687, Lully missed the floor and speared his toe by accident. The toe turned gangrenous, but Lully refused amputation and died.

- In all of history, there's never been anyone killed so many times as the mad monk Grigory Yefimovich Rasputin—a debauched and disreputable advisor to the Russian czar Nicholas II. His enemies poisoned him, then shot him. Still alive, he rushed them, and they shot him twice more. They kicked Rasputin in the head; they beat him bloody with a steel rod. That surely did him in, but just to be on the safe side, they bound him and dumped him into the icy Neva River. The autopsy later proved their decision right: The cold water had apparently revived the still-living Rasputin: he'd freed a hand and was trying to find a way to resurface before he finally drowned. Because of his powers to revive, revive, and revive again, the Bolsheviks dug up his grave several months later and set fire to his coffin, to make absolutely dead sure.

- Isadora Duncan, the larger-than-life modern dancer in the early 20th century, was killed by one of her own signature scarves. As she got into a little sports car in Nice, she hadn't noticed that the long, red scarf had trailed behind and gotten caught underneath the car wheel. As the driver sped off, the scarf wrapped itself around and around the axle. It tightened around her neck and killed her instantly. Isadora was pulled out of the car and dragged behind for several yards before anyone knew what had happened.

- Actress Jayne Mansfield was beheaded by a mosquito-spraying truck. Rushing late at night from Mississippi to Louisiana to make an appearance, the driver of her car rear-ended the truck while it was spraying the sleepy Southern towns along that stretch of highway. The car ended up under the truck, and Mansfield, her driver, and manager were all decapitated; in the backseat, her three sleeping children survived with only minor injuries.

Ask! How can I find locations of famous people's graves?